Acclaim for the stories of
*How TV Ruined My Sex Life
and a Bunch of Other Messed Up Misadventures*

How TV Ruined My Sex Life

I think your story is the "bomb"! - *Daniel Patrick McCormick*

It was hysterically funny. And entertaining. And readable. You have a great voice and a great style. - *Marsha Koretzky*

First Night Back

LOL!! An elderly woman sitting near me on the beach asked what I was reading that was so funny. "Nothing," I replied, hoping she'd go away as I wiped the tears from my eyes. - *James Barrett*

The Day I Created the Naked Monster

The writing here is definitely first class. - *James Barrett*

I read it once and smiled my way all thru it. I read it a second time and wished it (the story!!) were longer. - *Sita Bahskar*

The Airport Reading Material Incident

A bit of light-hearted fun, with a serious undercurrent of political statement on the current moral climate... - *Guy Koehler*

Some lines are so good they're practically quotable... - *Daniel S. Yu*

The Dog Don't Lie

Your story is the first one in quite a while that I actually wanted to finish... It's well written, it's funny, it's enjoyable. - *Maly Misio*

The Russian Bride

Man, I have been laughing for the past half an hour!
- *Juan Antonio Perez Gamez*

The Hair Bag

You set the tone of the story from the very first sentence, and I loved the stylistic way in which it was presented. I laughed several times at the clever set of circumstances you devised. Fun! Fun! Fun!
- *Anonymous, Literotica.com*

How TV Ruined My Sex Life

And a Bunch of Other Messed Up Misadventures

By

Vinny Smith

Published by Junkie Entertainment
Albuquerque, New Mexico

Printed in the United States of America
ISBN 978-0-6152-1628-7

For Jennie, who wonders where
this twisted stuff comes from
and for my mom
who I hope
never reads this book.

Table of Contents

How TV Ruined My Sex Life   7

The Hair Bag   17

The Dog Don't Lie   32

The Russian Bride   46

The Truth About the Chair   60

The Rock Star   74

High School (Reunion, Not a Musical)   89

The Day I Created the Naked Monster   105

The Airport Reading Material Incident   114

Two Very Different Dances   123

From Ecurse69   136

Trinity Spoiled   147

Chemistry   162

First Night Back   177

Sam Smells Sex   187

HOW TV RUINED MY SEX LIFE

I wish there was a way to not blame my parents for my TV addiction but I just haven't been able to find one. My earliest memory is of watching TV through the bars of my crib. I remember the safe feeling I got every afternoon at two o'clock when the brilliant glow from the lighthouse announced the beginning of the soap opera, *Guiding Light.* Come to think of it, I probably actually got hooked while still in the womb since my mother was hopelessly addicted to her soaps. Looking back, an in utero heroin addiction might have been better. And really, the only good thing about a TV addiction at age one is that you never have to worry about missing anything while you go to the bathroom; you just go right there on the spot, someone will deal with it during a commercial or when the smell gets bad enough.

Along with my sex life, which I'll get to in a second, it severely hampered my ability to hold a job, rather, a good job. I always sought out positions where I could watch TV. It didn't even have to be regular TV per se, whatever it was, just had to be on one. I took jobs in video stores or electronic stores, anywhere there was a TV. Hell, even my job at the fucking 7-11 had security monitors. I went to college and studied, you guessed it, TV production. That led me into jobs in master control, the part of the TV station where the job is to watch TV. The problem with that, though, is that not only is it the lowest paid and least respected job in a station, but it's also the first one to get hit with cutbacks. Needless to say, I was unemployed more than I wasn't.

I grew up in Austin, Texas, which is a huge music town. So captivating the tube was to me, that whenever I had backstage passes to a big concert, which was all the time, I would always end up watching the show on the closed circuit system rather than from the side of the stage or wherever. Sad, huh?

Guiding Light kept me hooked well into my twenties. In 1982, my first summer as a high school post-grad, however, was the year TV fucked up my sex life just as it should have been getting rolling. I place the blame squarely on *Guiding Light* for this although if it hadn't been that show, certainly another one would have done just as much damage. Summers in Austin were Africa-hot and Caribbean-sticky. Thank God we had a pool. And thank God most of my friends didn't. That meant that every summer there was a steady stream of nubile young ladies hanging out at my place. My parents worked long, fucked up hours so they weren't around much and my sister decided to spend the summer in California where she had just finished her junior year at Occidental College. I basically had the community pool and TV - life was good.

I was one of those guys that made friends easily (no, it wasn't just because I had a pool) and I found it particularly easy to make friends with the best looking girls, I just could never take it to the next level. I was into this girl, Mary, one of the hottest girls in school. To this day, she still ranks as the best hardbody I've ever seen. With a teardrop-shaped ass, ample breasts and long, dark hair, there wasn't a single thing I'd change about her. The thing that was interesting, though, was the stories I'd heard about her. This one not-particularly-good-looking jock-type talked about the time he almost fucked her but she was so tight he couldn't get it in. He was the one who dubbed her "Hairy Mary".

There was the rumor about the time she deep-throated, Johnny "Huge" Johnson, the legendary quarterback from UT. Reports had Johnny Huge at a hair over eleven inches. No small feat for a five-foot-two girl with an average-sized mouth. Then there was the time she got drunk and passed out at Joe Craiger's ten-kegger and wound up getting her pussy shaved by the baseball team. "Hairy Mary" briefly became "Bare-y Mary". Of course I missed the whole fucking thing because I had to leave early. Why? It was the season finale of *Dallas.*

Mary and I knew each other but didn't really hang around the same people. When I ran into her at the grocery store that sweltering Friday morning, pleasantries were exchanged and small talk ensued. I can't remember what she was buying but I was getting Pop Tarts and watermelon, my daily menu for *Guiding Light* viewing. It was close to a hundred fucking degrees at 10 am and would only get worse as the day wore on. For some reason it never occurred to me to invite her over for a swim but after she dropped a few not-so-subtle hints, I finally got it and gladly extended an invitation, as I tried to hold back a shit-eating grin.

"Great," she said sweetly. "Noon okay?"

My heart sank a little. "Oh... that late?" The ideal situation for me would have been for her to come over now, hang about three hours or so then get the fuck out by the time *Guiding Light* came on at 2.

"Yeah, I gotta take my little sister somewhere at 11:30 but then I'm free the rest of the day. Why, you got something else to do?" she asked.

"Actually, I have to be somewhere at 2."

The look on her face was one of confusion. "Okay, that's like two hours, that's plenty of time for a dip."

Fuck, first, that was a stupid comment on my part and second, that's half the time I could have spent with this half-naked girl alone in my yard. I tried to cover my idiocy. "Yeah, yeah, that's cool. See you at twelve then?"

On the way home I wondered what my chances of having sex with this girl would be. I'm not a bad looking guy, I'm smart and funny, why not me? Then I suddenly remembered that all of her wild sex stories involved jocks. I was just a guy who worked in a video store. I'd never played a sport in my life. Is that what the secret was? Being a fucking pumped up meathead? I didn't think I had a prayer. Besides, even if something were going to happen, it would have to be over by 2. I was going to have to settle for stealing looks and using my imagination later. Damn it. Why did she have to take her stupid little sister to wherever-the-fuck? It just wasn't fair.

It was 12:20 by the time she finally showed up. I was just starting to get annoyed as the clock drew further away from 12 and nearer to 2. She was apologetic and I played it off like it was no big deal. I pointed her toward my sister's room to change. I went outside and jumped in the pool. Now it was like a hundred-and-fucking-ten outside. The water felt great.

She emerged from the house in the tiniest, unbelievably sexy string bikini I'd ever seen. I got hard instantly. She took her time descending the three steps into the pool and allowed me a nice long gaze at her perfect body. She bent over backward to soak her hair, and I got an extended look at her breasts as they sat perched just above the water line.

The next hour was spent soaking and talking. It was the most time I'd ever spent with her and I was pleased to find out that she was down to earth and funny. The conversation eventually drifted toward sex and somehow settled on pornography. In 1982 VCR's hadn't yet exploded on the scene so porn was a lot less accessible than it is now. It was pretty much limited to movie theaters and magazines. Feeling kind of gutsy, I mentioned that I had a small collection of *Playboy* magazines but it was actually dwarfed in size by my sister's *Playgirl* collection.

"Really?" she said, perking up.

"Oh yeah," I said. "Want to see them?"

"What do you think?"

Next thing I knew, I was digging through my sister's porn stash in the trunk at the foot of her bed. Now, I had been down this road before and vowed to myself I would never snoop through her shit again. It was just after she had come home for the summer after her first year in college and seemed to have more cash than usual. Naturally I didn't think she'd miss a little so one afternoon I went looking for it. I got into the trunk and saw the *Playgirl* collection but also, strangely enough, an issue of *Hustler* magazine. I perused the pages and got a lot more than I bargained for. Apparently *Hustler* had discovered her after her boyfriend submitted a naked polaroid for their *Girl Next Door* search. Now there she was with her own "spread". And spread she was, spread so wide I swear you could practically see her pancreas. The funniest thing was that she'd spent all of her high school years trying to convince people that she was a natural blonde.

Now the world knew the truth. I could only stare at the photos for about fifteen minutes before my disgust got the better of me. I never did find any money.

So there I was again, dreading what I might find. My attention was soon diverted back to Mary who had wasted no time in finding an issue to thumb through. I looked at my watch. It was 1:30 and show time was rapidly approaching. She found a nice roll of beefcake to show me, which really only served to make me feel inadequate. I really didn't want to see those huge guys lying there all flopped over like that.

"That's nice," I said, regretting my decision to show her that stuff.

"He reminds me of this football player I once knew." She put that issue down, grabbed another and hopped up to the bed. She sat Indian-style and laid out the magazine in front of her.

"I gotta go in like twenty minutes," I said sheepishly.

"Uh huh," she said with indifference.

It was then that I caught a glimpse at her crotch area. Her tiny little bikini bottoms were riding up into her pussy. Apparently the hair had grown back after the Joe Craiger ten-kegger shaving incident. Her clit had escaped the tight confines of her lycra bottoms and I could not believe she didn't notice. Once again, I got hard instantly.

It seemed like I stared at it for an hour, though it was only a couple of seconds. My eyes went from her bush to her face, which, to my horror, was staring right back at me. "Whatcha lookin' at?" she asked expressionless.

My heart dropped into my gut. I was fucking caught. I could feel blackness enveloping my brain. My knees went weak. "What?" I squeaked.

"You heard me."

"I.... uh... I..."

She looked down at her crotch then looked back up at me without doing anything about the exposure.

"Well?" She looked pissed.

"Sorry... I... uh... uh...

"You get a good look?"

"I wasn't... I... um...

Then she did the unthinkable. "Does this help?" She straightened out her legs and spread them. I was getting a phenomenal look. A sly smile crossed her face.

"Yeah..." I said, stunned. I couldn't move.

"How about now?" She stuck her finger into the corner of the suit and pulled it completely away, giving me the full view. I didn't know what to do. I couldn't talk; I felt funny staring, so I glanced over at the clock radio. It read 1:45.

"You want to touch it?"

"Yes," I said, barely audible.

She pulled at the strings on either side of the suit and removed it completely. Jesus Christ! I could practically feel the fucking heart attack coming on! Next she removed her top. The hottest girl I'd ever seen was lying there naked on my sister's bed!

She laid back and spread her legs a little more. "Give me your hand."

I inched toward her and did as I was told. She took hold of my hand and used it to help pull her back toward me. I got down on my knees next to the bed. She placed my hand squarely on her bush. I spread my fingers and she guided them through the softest, thickest patch of hair I'd touched before or since. Hello Hairy Mary.

She took hold of my middle finger, moved it down until it reached her clit then used it to masturbate. I glanced at the clock again. 1:51. She turned my hand palm up and inserted my finger into her pussy until it wouldn't go any further. I shot a load in my swim trunks.

I started to fuck her with that lucky digit. Slow in and out strokes, gradually picking up speed. She rubbed her clit faster and faster and moaned with every in-stroke. I added my index finger. It had to be two hundred degrees inside her. She let out a scream and pussy juice free-flowed. I couldn't breathe. 1:54.

I withdrew my fingers and before I could do anything else, she sat up and took my hand again. She put my fingers in her mouth and sucked them dry. "I love the taste, don't you?" She asked.

"Well, I..."

"Taste me."

"Huh?"

"Go ahead."

She grabbed me behind my head and pulled me between her legs. On the way down I noticed it was 1:56. I pulled away. "You have to go."

The look on her face was one of pure shock. "Excuse me?"

"I told you I have to be somewhere by 2."

"Looks like you're going to be late," she said sarcastically.

"I know that's why you have to go now."

"You're serious? Where do you have to go?"

I had to think of something quick. I never, ever figured I'd be in a situation like this. "I gotta go do this thing for this guy." I cringed. Jesus, that was fucking lame.

"What thing? For who?"

"You don't know him." I stood up and looked at the glaring 1:57 on the clock. "Really, you've got to go." I held out my hand to help her off the bed. She just stared at me in bewilderment.

"Really," I repeated. Now I was going to have to toast the Pop-Tarts during a commercial instead of having them ready at the beginning. I always had the Pop-Tarts promptly at 2 then I'd have the watermelon at 2:30, just as the second half was starting. I advanced my hand a little closer. She finally got that I was serious. She slapped my hand away and stood up on her own. "Unbelievable," she said. "Un-fucking-believable."

What could I say? You just can't miss the Friday episode of a soap. Everybody knows they have cliffhangers on Fridays. I shifted my weight from one foot to the other. Now I had to piss and I was going to have to wait until the first commercial break meaning that I wouldn't be able to toast the Pop-Tarts until break two. My afternoon was quickly getting pretty fucked up.

I watched her as she gathered up her clothes. She pulled on her panties and shot me the "stink-eye". "You mind getting the fuck out of here while I get dressed?"

"Sorry." I left the room and waited impatiently in the hall. I could see the grandfather clock in the den. It was 1:58. It sure seemed like she was taking her sweet-ass time.

She finally came out at 1:59, fully clothed and not in a good mood. She brushed past me toward the front door. "So maybe we can do this again sometime?" I asked hopefully.

"Right," she snapped. And with that she was out the door. Finally. The cuckoo clock in the living room announced the two o'clock hour. All right! Here we go! I flipped on the TV, turned the knob to channel 5 and parked myself in my favorite chair. But what I saw wasn't *Guiding Light*. It was Dan Fucking Rather pre-empting the show to bring us a live press conference with President Fucking Reagan! Oh my God! Were they shitting me? It was on every channel. I couldn't even flip over to my backup show, *Days of Our Lives*. I kicked the TV and went to go take that piss. In the words of Hairy Mary: un-fucking-believable.

So that was the beginning of the end of my sex life. I wish I could say I changed after that, but I didn't. There were many more incidents just like that as the years went by. Eventually I got a VCR and later a TiVo and that alleviated some of the problems but I still put what's on that beautiful glowing box above everything else. Today, I still watch *Guiding Light* but for years I refused to watch Dan Rather. I also refused to vote for Reagan in '84. Yeah, I'm still single, if I want sex I have to pay for it, and I have trouble lifting my growing fat ass out of the La-Z-Boy. Thanks, Mom. Thanks, Dad. Thanks, boob tube.

THE HAIR BAG

Gavin Thompson had the cleanest bathroom in America. You could actually eat off the toilet seat it was so clean. Not that you'd really want to even if you did have the opportunity. For Gavin, cleaning the bathroom was therapy and he seemed to need a lot of therapy. He cleaned it once a day, every day, including holidays. Sometimes he'd even do it twice.

He had a two bedroom, two bath corner condo unit with the only roof garden in the building. It opened up to a spectacular view of the Rocky Mountains. It was definitely one of the best views from any building in Boulder. For a budding novelist it was an ideal spot to write. The view provided him with plenty of inspiration. It was also the perfect spot for romantic dinners. It was a grand idea that he was not able to pull off very often. In fact, he'd only had one dinner on the roof garden and that was with his best friend, Tina. Hardly the romantic situation he'd hoped for. His roommate, Steve, on the other hand, used it all the time. When the weather was good, Steve would have dinner out there with a different girl at least three times a week. The sounds of wild sex coming from Steve's room would usually follow. That never bothered Gavin. In fact, he looked forward to listening to it.

Gavin was a chronic masturbator so each of Steve's conquests provided him with plenty of material. Gavin would make sure and meet each one when they first came over and then would quickly retreat to his room to jerk off. If he could squirt one out right away it gave him at least two hours to rejuvenate before the after dinner sex would happen and he could give it a whack again. Gavin also had a fetish. He was absolutely crazy for pussy hair.

Many days he spent more time searching for porn on the internet than he did actual writing. He had found hundreds of hairy pussy websites and had downloaded more than 96,000 photos to his computer. With that many women in his archive it made it fairly easy to find a few that looked a lot like pretty much any girl Steve brought home. He would jerk off then take the time to search, copy, rename the photos with the name of the girl he'd just met and re-file them in the "Steve" folder. That way he always had a memory and they always had hairy pussies no matter whether they shaved or waxed them in real life or not. This almost always caused feelings of guilt and stress which, in turn, caused him to go scrub down his bathroom. That is how he got the cleanest bathroom in America.

Gavin never wanted a roommate but as a sometimes-struggling writer, he wasn't always able to swing the mortgage payment by himself. He'd met Steve during the one month he had actually used the one year membership to the gym around the corner. He'd bought that with the advance on his yet-to-be-started second novel. He'd also paid cash for a new Toyota Prius, bought the latest in flat screen and home theater technology for his living room and all new furniture that did not come from IKEA this time so he would not have to assemble it himself.   After all was spent and done, he came to the disturbing realization that it might be a while before he got any decent royalty checks from his first novel that wasn't exactly tearing up the best seller lists.

Gavin had casually mentioned to Steve, a personal trainer at the gym, that he was looking for a dependable roommate.   After much discussion, and assurances from Steve that he wasn't going to dirty up the place, it was agreed that he would move in on a month-to-month basis.   So far it had worked out great; Steve had held up his end of the bargain and kept the common areas clean.   He also kept his doors shut so if he actually did make a mess in his own bedroom or bathroom, Gavin would never know.   They respected each other's space, stayed out of each other's stuff and pretty much lived their own separate lives.

As far as Gavin's own sex life was concerned, there wasn't much to speak of.   He was hung up on someone he couldn't have so he became content with jerking off to his hairy pussy files.   He would simply wait until either his soulmate came along and found him or he could actually have the one he wanted.   That one was his best friend, Tina.

It had been six years since he'd tried to make a move on her and had taken no chances with her or anyone else since.   Gavin and Tina had been best friends since their senior year in high school until, finally, three sexually frustrating years later, he felt that the time was finally right to take their friendship to the next level.   He dressed up in his best suit and sat down at their favorite table at their favorite sports bar with an awesome view of the Rockies.   He just knew it was going to be a special night.

"Wow, you're all spiffy," she said, as she walked up wearing casual clothes and a big smile on her face. "What's the occasion? I'm obviously not dressed for it, whatever it is. I thought we were just meeting for happy hour." She gave him a quick peck on the lips.

"Well, I'm pretty happy," he said.

"Yeah? Me too, actually."

Gavin pulled out her chair for her then sat back down. "Good. I have something important I want to talk to you about," he said, taking a serious tone.

"Really?" That's so funny; I have something I want to talk to you about also."

"Wow. Great minds, huh?"

"Exactly. You go first," she said.

"No, that's okay, you go.

"Okay!" she said, bursting with excitement. "I have wanted to tell you this for so long. I was just scared about how you'd feel but so much time has gone by now, I feel I can finally tell you what I've been wanting to for so long." She placed her hands over his, her face absolutely beaming. "You know how sometimes in life you can search and search and not realize that what you wanted all along is right under your nose?"

Gavin couldn't speak. He couldn't believe it; she was in love with him too. He was finally going to be with the woman of his dreams. He just nodded and hoped that his racing heart wouldn't jump through his chest.

"Wow. I can't believe I'm about to say this."

Gavin leaned forward. He was all ears. "It's been so many years... Now that I think about it, I guess I've known since high school..." she said.

"Yes," Gavin squeaked.

"I don't know how to say this." She wiped away a happy tear. "I told myself I wouldn't get nervous."

"Go ahead, just say it." Gavin's mouth was open... waiting.

"Okay, here goes," she said. The pause in between sentences seemed to take forever. "I'm a lesbian!" she blurted out for the entire place to hear.

A chill ran through his entire body. No matter what he did, he could not close his mouth. "Gavin? Did you hear me? You okay? Gavin? Gavin?" That was the last thing he heard before he passed out.

Six years later he still carried a torch for her and although he'd never seen her naked, he imagined her that way - thick, black, hairy bush and all - for the first jerk off of every day.

****

"I have a huge favor to ask," Tina said, putting on the smile that would assure she would get whatever she wanted from Gavin.

"What's that?" he asked, as he handed her the popcorn and joined her on the couch in front of the big screen.

"You know how I started going to the gym around the corner?"

"Yeah."

"Well, the place is awesome but the showers are kind of nasty."

"So, why don't you tell Steve and see if there's something he can do?"

"He said they're going to renovate them next year so they won't do anything now."

"Sucks for you."

"Well, that's where you come in. I was hoping you'd let me come up and use yours until then," she said, batting her eyes playfully. "I know it's a total pain in the ass."

The thought of Tina naked in his bathroom gave him an instant boner. "I guess," he said, trying to act like he couldn't care less. "Use your key if I'm not here." And leave the bathroom door open if I am, he thought.

****

Gavin was feeling especially guilty. Steve's date from the night before was incredibly hot - hotter than usual. He had taken extra special care cleaning the bathroom after that. He also knew Tina was coming over so that provided some extra incentive to do an extra special job. He was bummed that he was going to miss her first shower because he had to be at a lunch meeting with his editor. At least a lunch meeting was better than what he usually did around that time of day, which was walk. He needed to get some sort of exercise since the gym thing hadn't worked out. Now he was going to have to change his routine around so he could try to be available in case Tina needed anything for her showers. Oh well, there were going to be plenty of them, he could miss this one.

****

After his lunch meeting Gavin came home and went straight to his room. He was all set to jerk off while he visualized his editor. She looked pretty good for a woman in her fifties and had really thick eyebrows which, in Gavin's mind, signified the presence of a nice, bushy muff.

He went into the bathroom to wash his hands because he could still smell the soy sauce he had spilled. He reached for the towel and happened to look down into the tub. That's when he saw it. Right there, two inches from the drain was a crooked, black hair. The towel fell to the floor and he dropped to his knees. "Holy shit," he said out loud. "No fucking way!" He reached down and picked it up. The analysis was quick.

He was able to rule himself out right away. First of all, Gavin was blond and this hair was most definitely black. Just like Tina's hair. It was about an inch long; too long to be from an eyebrow or, God forbid, the nose. It couldn't be from an armpit. Tina wore tank tops a lot and he knew she shaved under there. It was too short and scraggly to be from her head; she had long, flowing hair. It could be from her ass, but even if it was, that was kind of a turn on too. No, it had to be a pussy hair, it just had to be.

He closed the drain in the sink, gently placed the hair in it and slowly backed away. He didn't want to take any chance of losing his precious find. He went around the apartment, gathered up a few items and hurried back to his bathroom. First, he set up the little lamp he'd taken from his desk then produced the magnifying glass his grandfather had given him as a kid. He stared, fascinated, at the hair in the good light for at least fifteen minutes before digging out the sandwich-sized ziplock bag he'd shoved in his pocket. He dropped the hair into the bag, sealed it up tight and held it under the light. Then he dropped his pants, set free the hardest cock he'd ever had, and with two strokes, shot semen all over the front of his vanity. His knees went weak and he had to brace himself. It was the single-most intense orgasm he'd ever had.

Gavin sat down on the floor exhausted. He continued to stare at the hair for a few more moments before he got the brilliant idea to scour the shower for more. He was delighted to find two more in the tub and another one on the soap. Four total. It was like he'd discovered his own personal oil strike - one that would provide many more gushers in the future.

This went on for a year. Gavin had all but abandoned the "Steve" file and concentrated solely on filling what he called "the hair bag." Every day he found three or four hairs in the shower and a couple more on the floor where Tina would obviously shed again during the drying process. The bag was looking good. He had stopped counting the hairs after about a month but now he had collected a nice mound of hair that was moldable and shapeable. At least twice a day he closed the drain in the sink and emptied the bag into the basin. He would then shape the hair into a perfect triangle and jerk off while staring at it. Sometimes he would take a handful and rub it all over his cock, imagining what it would feel like to plow it across her thick, bushy pussy. Once in a while, he would even lay it out on his face and flick his tongue at it, as if they were in a sixty-nine. It was a damn good time for Gavin. At least until the day tragedy struck.

****

"You want a little more coffee?" Gavin asked Tina.

"Nah, I'm heading over to the gym. That'll just add to my water weight, then I'll feel fat. That'll just make me want to work harder, then that'll make me drink more liquid. It'll be this whole vicious cycle thing," she said.

"Wow. I thought I had issues. You could have just stopped at 'nah'."

They both laughed. "So I guess I'll see you back here about 12:30 to shower then," he said.

"Actually, no." She stood up to leave. "Didn't you hear? They're opening the new locker room facilities today. I'm finally going to stop being an obnoxious pest and shower at the gym from now on."

Gavin turned a sickly shade of white. "No, I hadn't heard."

"I can't believe Steve didn't tell you. I know you hardly ever see him but I thought he might have mentioned it. Anyway, I don't know how I'll ever repay you for your hospitality for the last - what's it been - a year? I really can't thank you enough. I want to do something special for you."

He was in a state of shock. He stared right through her and didn't hear a word. "Gavin? Gavin? Did you hear me?"

She grabbed his shoulders and shook him. He came out of it and tried to not look like his entire world had just been rocked. "Uh... yeah... sure. Uh, you know you can keep using it. It's no bother at all. In fact, those showers over there are probably going to get funked up pretty quickly so if I were you, I'd still use this one. At least you know it'll be clean, right?"

"Freakishly clean," she laughed. "It's okay, I've imposed enough. I'll see you later." She kissed him on the cheek and headed out to the hallway.

He followed her as far as the door. He called down the hall in desperation. "It's okay... seriously!"

She waved and disappeared down the stairs.

He started to dry heave. It was time for therapy. It was time to clean the bathroom.

****

After scrubbing his bathroom from top to bottom, Gavin pulled out the bag of pussy hair from the waterproof/fireproof safe he had bought to exclusively house the bag. This would be one of those "once in a whiles" where he buried his face in Tina's pubes. He brought the bag into the bathroom and opened it up. He took a long satisfying whiff. In reality there was no odor of any kind but in Gavin's mind there was a slight sweet and soapy/fishy smell. Surely it was exactly what she smelled like down there right after showering and prancing around his bathroom naked.

He dropped his pants then stuck his hand in the bag and pulled out a generous handful. He molded it into a triangular shape and held it in his hand. He closed his eyes, licked it and imagined he was licking her clit. He grabbed onto his cock and started to stroke.

"Oh my God! What are you doing?" Tina shrieked.

"Shit!" Gavin screamed, as the hair went flying. He yanked his pants up as quickly as he could. "What are you doing here?"

"The new locker room got flooded so I came to use the shower."

"So you just walk in? You don't knock?" He zipped up.

"That's what I've done for a year! What the *fuck* is that?" she asked, horrified. The pussy-shaped mound of hair had landed on the floor nearly intact. What wasn't on the floor was stuck to his white-as-a-sheet face.

"It's nothing," he stuttered while he gathered up what he could and closed it up in his fist.

"Bullshit. Is that what I think it is?"

"I... I... just shaved; I was just... cleaning up."

"That is such a lie," she said as she grabbed the hair bag off the sink for a closer look.

Gavin made a grab for it. "Gimme it, Goddamn it!"

She turned away and opened it. She pulled some hair out and rubbed it around in her hands. "This is pubic hair," she observed.

"I don't know what you're talking about. Give it here," he said holding out his other hand.

"Why in the hell do you have a bag of pubic hair?"

"I don't. Give it."

"There's some on your face."

He wiped it off, not caring to gather it up.

"Whose hair is this? I'm not giving it back until you tell me."

"Jesus. Come on."

"I want to know."

Gavin let out a deep breath and hung his head in defeat. This was going to be the single hardest and absolute worst conversation he was ever going to have. He had no idea what her reaction would be. After her initial shocked response, she seemed to be acting normal. Honesty was the best policy he decided. If he couldn't trust his best friend, who could he trust? He had held it in long enough. Today would be the day that he finally told her how he felt about her and it would be a huge weight off his shoulders. His biggest fear was that she would get mad and never speak to him again. He *had* to overcome the fear and embarrassment. Now was the time. "Okay fine," he said. "I'll tell you everything."

****

Tina sat on the edge of his bed and listened intently to Gavin's confessions for the entire fifteen minutes. He poured his guts out about how he'd been in love with her since high school and about how he had the pubic hair fetish ever since he found his father's *Playboy* collection when he was ten. It was all so hard to hear. She was sorry she'd forced him to tell his story. She was not prepared either emotionally or intellectually to deal with the ramifications of his revelations. She had seen deep into the soul of someone whom she thought she knew inside and out and now wasn't sure she ever knew him at all.

"So that's it," Gavin said. "I just don't want you to be mad, that's all."

"Mad? I have no reason to be mad. Disturbed? Maybe. Flattered? Absolutely. Confused? Definitely."

"Okay," Gavin said sheepishly, not knowing what the confusion was about.

"Obviously, I understand the feelings for me. I mean come on, look at me. Who wouldn't love this? The fetish thing, I have to say, is a little weird. But hey, who's not a little weird, right?"

"Exactly," Gavin said, perking up.

"The thing I still don't get though, is whose hair is in the bag?"

Now he was the one who was confused. "I thought that was obvious."

"Not so much."

"It's yours. I've been gathering it from the shower ever since you've been using it."

She just looked at him expressionless for a moment.

"What?" he asked. "Say something."

"Wow," she said, still with no expression.

He started to get nervous. Wow sounded bad. I crossed the line, he thought. It was all good until now. Until wow. Please God, let it be okay.

"Wow," she said again. "You just have no idea, do you?"

"I don't know."

She got up from the bed shaking her head. "Well, I gotta tell you, I don't think you're going to want to hear what I have to say," she said in a somber voice.

Gavin started to sweat. Shit, I knew it, he thought. I fucked up big time. "Please. I am so sorry."

"Hey, don't apologize to me, Tina said pointing to the hair bag. "Apologize to whoever's hair that is."

"What are you talking about? It's yours."

"Uh, no. Let's just say if I lived in Brazil I'd fit right in."

"Huh?"

"Geez, do I have to spell everything out? It's called a Brazilian wax. It strips away all the hair."

Gavin winced at the thought.

"I haven't had hair down there since I was like, nineteen," she laughed. "Since about the time I told you I was gay; which I still very much am, by the way."

A sharp pain shot through Gavin's brain and he could feel breakfast rumble in his gut. "Bullshit."

"It's true. I'd show you but, well you know... Who knows what you would do with *that* visual?"

He slumped down onto the bed as his world spun around him. "I don't get it. Where the hell did it come from then?"

Just then Steve appeared at the door with a towel and a box full of manscaping products. "Whoa, sorry dude, I didn't know you were home," he said.

"What difference would that make?" Gavin asked.

"I was going to shower."

"So go shower."

"Nah, you guys are busy, I'll come back."

"Come back for what?" Gavin asked.

"Oh God," Tina said as she turned away and covered her mouth to keep from laughing.

"The shower," Steve said.

"You have your own shower."

"Oh I never use mine, it's way too nasty. Yours is always so nice and clean."

Tina could not contain herself any longer. She laughed so hard she couldn't catch her breath.

"Oh God," Gavin choked as he caught on. "How long have you been using it? Please don't say a year."

"That's about right."

Gavin began to dry heave.

Tina fell on the floor and kicked her legs in the air. She had tears in her eyes from laughing so hard.

Steve looked back and forth at Tina and Gavin. He was totally confused. "What?" he said, trying to get an answer from anyone.

Gavin finished heaving then jumped up from the bed and screamed for Steve to get out.

Steve had never seen or heard Gavin raise his voice and frankly, it kind of scared him. He took the cue and quickly left.

Gavin turned his attention to Tina. He was embarrassed beyond belief. "You too. Get the fuck out!"

She was finally able to catch her breath as her laughter subsided. "Don't yell at me. This is all you," she said.

"Go," he said pointing at the door. The tables had turned. At the moment he couldn't care less whether or not she ever spoke to him again. He just wanted her and the embarrassment to go away. He sat back down and hung his head.

She stood up. She truly felt bad for him. She tried to approach him but he waved her off. "Please just go," he said calmly.

"It's all going to be okay," she said. "Call me when you feel like talking."

She left and closed the door behind her. Gavin sat still for a moment then looked over at the bag of hair next to him. He shook his head in disbelief then walked the bag into the bathroom. He emptied every little bit of it into the toilet and flushed it away forever. He discarded the ziplock bag into the trash then stood and looked at himself in the mirror for a moment. His agenda for the rest of the afternoon was becoming crystal clear. First he was going to jerk off while he imagined licking Tina's freshly waxed, completely bald pussy now that he knew for sure what it looked like. Then he was going to clean his bathroom like he never had before.

THE DOG DON'T LIE

They had been going at it hard for only twelve minutes. It was a monumental occasion in Tom and Julia's sex life. After nine months of dating he had finally persuaded her to let him give it to her up the ass. She'd surprised him with only two conditions. First, he must wear a condom and second, if it hurt too much he'd have to stop. No problem, he thought. He even brought over a brand new box of condoms that were designed to enhance her pleasure and a Costco-sized bottle of Boy Butter lubricant.

They were both sweating profusely and Julia, as Tom assured her she would, seemed to be enjoying it. He was a little disappointed that she wasn't going to get to see his cum face. He just knew this one was going to be intense and probably contort his face until he was virtually unrecognizable.

He was thirty seconds from exploding when suddenly her dog, a ragged but sweet old mutt named Hank, began barking bloody murder in the living room. Julia instantly stopped moving. Tom couldn't care less. Whatever it was that had gotten Hank started could wait. He tried to keep pumping but when she elbowed him in the cheek and ordered him to stop in a loud whisper, he did exactly what he was told.

They listened until they heard the sliding front door of her double-wide slam, then they scrambled. Tom pulled out, rolled off of her and gathered up his clothes. Julia worked frantically to straighten up the bed. They could hear Julia's ex-husband, Jimmy, call her name as he approached the back bedroom. Tom headed for the window. Julia grabbed a towel from the bathroom. As Tom climbed out, he turned and noticed the condom was hanging out of her ass.

"Baby," he whispered. "It's still in your ass!"

She shot him a look that strongly suggested that he'd better both shut up *and* get out.

"The condom. It's still in your ass!" Tom repeated.

She could hear Jimmy coming down the hall. She felt around and yanked the condom out. She flung it in the direction of the waste basket near the closet and wrapped herself in the towel. Tom fell into the junipers just as Jimmy and the excited dog came through the bedroom door.

In Tom's mind all the sneaking around and all the drama was totally unnecessary, after all, Julia and Jimmy's divorce had been final for a good six months. By all accounts, Julia had a right to do whatever she wanted now that she was free - including taking it up the ass at 1:30 on a Friday afternoon if she so chose. The problem was Julia was afraid of how Jimmy might react to the news. According to her, he was quite emotionally fragile. Tom had never met him and had no idea if it was true.

Tom had heard numerous stories that all ended with Jimmy getting his skinny ass kicked in the parking lot of some bar because he'd gotten too drunk and latched on to some poor random sap who just wanted to drink his beer in peace. Jimmy would pour his heart out and cry, "I love you man." He was always crying over something; losing his woman, losing his job, whatever. Imagine a guy that looks like a 1970's carnival worker complete with skintight bell-bottom jeans, long, stringy hair and a horseshoe mustache, bleeding, bawling, and crawling home every night. Drunk or sober, it didn't matter, the man was a crier.

Tom probably should have felt sorry for him; he just didn't. Julia did though, and now for the third time in the nine months they had been dating, Tom found himself naked in the bushes under Julia's bedroom window clutching his clothes in a ball. It was bad enough that she made Tom park in visitors parking. There was plenty of room to pull into her driveway and park behind her but since her trailer was visible from the main road that Jimmy drove every day to work and back, she was afraid that he would see a strange truck there and launch first into an inquest, then into a cry-fest.

Tom lay there and thought both about how he needed to have a serious talk with Julia about this situation and how he needed, at thirty-five, to finally move out of his mother's cramped apartment and get his own place. While he sat and pondered, he saw Hank escape through the doggie door and head for the birdbath behind the trailer owned by the muumuu-wearing fat lady next door. He sniffed around, lifted his leg and pissed all over it.

Hank, of course, was the reason Jimmy was there in the first place. This was Jimmy's weekend for visitation. The dog was the closest thing Julia and Jimmy had to a kid and they shared custody as if he was. Jimmy had lost so much it would kill him if he lost his dog too, Julia had explained way too many times.

More often than not, Jimmy was late for the pick up so Tom and Julia figured there was plenty of time for sex. They were wrong. It was a hell of a time for Jimmy to become less predictable.

"You're crazy," Tom heard Julia say to Jimmy. "Of course I'm alone."

Those words always stung.

"And even if I wasn't, it's not really any of your business."

Jimmy took a suspicious look around the room. "Why didn't you answer when I called your name?"

"I was in the shower."

"Your hair's not wet."

"I mean I was about to get in the shower."

Tom hated Jimmy's inquisitions. Julia was always complaining about Jimmy butting into her business. Tom again looked over at Hank who was now apparently enjoying an afternoon snack of one of his own dried turds. Jesus, he thought, that dog would eat absolutely anything.

Tom realized the conversation had stopped. He was just about to try to peek into the window when suddenly Julia spoke up. "What the fuck are you looking at?"

Tom was startled. He dropped back down to the ground.

"You," Jimmy said. "You better not be lying to me."

"You're really starting to piss me off," she said. "Why don't you just get Hank and get the hell out of here."

He had started to piss Tom off too. It was all he could do to not jump through the window and knock the shit out of Jimmy.

"Oooh, you know how I like it when you talk like that. How about a quickie for old times sake?" He moved toward her.

"How about you go fuck yourself?"

"That's what I'm talking about. Now I'm really getting hot."

"Stay away from me."

Tom stood straight up. He was going to have to beat Jimmy to a bloody pulp.

Just then, Hank bounded back into the room and jumped into Jimmy's arms. He licked Jimmy's face like a little kid with an ice cream cone. It didn't strike Tom as funny at the moment, but later on he and Julia would laugh at the fact that Jimmy had gotten his face licked right after Hank had just come in from chowing down on a piece of shit.

Julia saw Tom at the window and waved for him to get down. He reluctantly did as she ordered. A juniper branch tried to scratch its way up his ass.

"At least Hank would never lie to me, would you boy?" Hank's lick-fest went into overdrive.

"Okay, why don't you take the party back to your own place."

"Fine, whatever. I'll bring him back Sunday afternoon."

"Try calling first for a change," she said.

"Fat chance," Tom whispered under his breath.

Tom waited until he heard Jimmy fire up his '74 Ford Ranchero (the uncool version of the awesome Chevy El Camino) and speed away before he stood to put his pants on. When he did, he spotted the fat lady next door as she smoked and watched him from her screened-in porch. Her stare was cut short when her even fatter boyfriend appeared behind her in nothing but his tighty-whities. Fat lady's boyfriend firmly planted his two giant ape-hands squarely on her ass. She giggled like a teenager crushed out her cigarette and went back inside. Then fat lady's boyfriend gave Tom two giant ape-thumbs up and went inside. Tom smiled sheepishly and bolted for Julia's front door.

The Dog Don't Lie

****

If Jimmy had not had his usual drunken, crying Friday night at the bar, he might never have seen it. Then again, his trailer was a disgusting garbage dump anyway, so he may very well not have seen it until it was too late.

Hank had tried his best not to shit on the kitchen floor, he really did. He had tried to get Jimmy's attention for hours. He barked at him, tugged at his bell-bottom cuff and even licked all the blood off of Jimmy's face. Nothing could roust him from the deep sleep and the green, vinyl la-z-boy he had collapsed into. He'd gone on a hell of a bender and wound up getting punched in the face twice.

Hank had no way to get out of the house to do his business and therefore had no choice but to let one drop on the cracked twenty-two year-old linoleum. That was around 10 am. By 2 pm it was really starting to ripen. It was a hot day and despite the fact that every window was open, it was well past ninety inside.

Around three, the booze wore off and amid the temperature and stink, Jimmy finally lifted his eyelids and took a blurry look around. As usual he didn't remember a thing about the previous night. He didn't know why his shirt and shoes were missing. He also couldn't figure out why his pants were unbuttoned but it reminded him of that time as a child when he'd had a tooth pulled and woke up from the gas with his pants in the same condition. He didn't notice the smell right away because something always smelled at his place. He spotted Hank curled up in a tight ball up against the back door. Jimmy called out to him, "Hank. C'mere boy."

Hank covered his eyes with his paws as if that would make him invisible. Every time he'd had an accident in Jimmy's trailer in the past he'd gotten yelled at and smacked on the nose with a magazine. Of course, the accidents were always due to Jimmy's irresponsibility.

As Jimmy slowly stood, he could feel the flesh of his back that had long ago fused itself to the chair with the help of heat and sweat, rip away from the vinyl. He screamed out in pain. For anyone else it would have been no big deal but for the overdramatic, oversensitive Jimmy, it was quite painful. He rubbed his back for a moment and cringed when he hit the spot that had torn away from the chair.

It was then that he recognized the distinctive smell of dog shit. His first thought was to check his feet. Nothing. That could only mean one thing: Hank had squeezed one out in the house. This infuriated Jimmy. "Hank, come here Godammit!"

Hank lowered his paws just enough to watch Jimmy come toward him.

Jimmy grabbed a *Hustler* off the counter and rolled it up. He had almost reached Hank when he saw the source of the offending odor. On the floor right smack in front of the sink was the nice, wet pile. "Oh, what the *fuck?*" The *Hustler* fell to the floor

He bent over and took a closer look. But it wasn't the pile itself he had screamed "what the *fuck?*" at. It happened to be what was twisted up in it. Nestled nicely in and around the brown goop was the condom that just twenty-six hours ago had been shoved way up Julia's ass. He reached down and pulled the condom out, paying no mind to the disgusting mass it was buried in and held it up to the light. There was still semen in the tip. "That lying *whore!*" he screamed.

Since he hadn't had sex with a human in a while, he instantly concluded that the only other place Hank could possibly have picked up a used condom was at Julia's place and if that was the case then she *must* be fucking somebody.

Jimmy shoved the shit-covered rubber in his pocket and headed for the front door. He called for Hank but not knowing if he was going to walk into a nose-smack, the dog hesitated. "Okay, fine. You want to sit here and smell your own shit all day, go ahead!" And with that he was gone without bothering to put on shoes or a shirt or to properly shut the door.

****

Tom was making the half-mile walk from Julia's back to visitors parking. There was a happy skip in his step. After Jimmy had left yesterday and after Tom complained about the situation for the umpteenth time he and Julia finally had been able to resume the rump-fuck. In fact, Julia had found it so enjoyable, she'd actually let Tom tap her ass two more times after that. Tom was a little sad though, that she had now declared a temporary moratorium on blow-jobs until she could get over the thought of sucking on something that had been in her ass a bunch of times. He had promised to shower and scrub his cock with bleach or something – whatever it took – both before and after they did the deed, whatever that deed happened to be. She said she'd get back to him on that. Other than that though, Tom was a happy guy. That was, at least until Jimmy sped by him doing 25 mph in the park's 8 mph zone as he headed toward Julia's trailer. What's this bullshit all about, he wondered. He turned and headed back to Julia's. The closer he got, the more pissed he got.

****

Julia had just stepped out of the shower when Jimmy burst in and caught her in all her nakedness. Julia freaked. "Jesus fucking Christ, Jimmy!" She quickly wrapped up in a towel. "What the *fuck* are you doing here?"

He yanked the shitty condom from his pocket and held it up inches from her face. "I think the better question is what the fuck are *you doing* here?"

"Ugh. What's that thing?" she said as she cringed and pulled away. "Get that away from me."

"It doesn't look familiar to you?"

"Why would it?"

"Because Hank crapped it out on my kitchen floor, that's why."

Julia suddenly flashed back to the condom she had tossed at the bedroom trash can and vaguely remembered missing it. "I've seen your floor, I'm surprised you even noticed," she said with a nervous laugh.

"That's right, laugh it up but I know you've been lying to me and I know you've been fucking someone!"

****

Jimmy had barely been gone two minutes when Hank decided it was time to head back home to Julia's. Before he left though, he raided the overflowing kitchen trash can, emptying the contents all over the floor. He found some nice pizza crust, a half-full can of tuna, some mac and cheese and of course the pile of poop. In his wake he left the kitchen a complete and total disaster area. Jimmy would probably never notice.

****

"So Hank picks up a condom somewhere and you automatically assume it came from here?" Julia asked, very annoyed.

"Where the hell else would it come from?"

"Well, first of all, he runs loose all over the park. He could have gotten it out of anyone's trash. And second of all, even if he did get it from here, we're divorced!" she yelled. "I can fuck who I want, when I want for as long as I want! So don't come in here and tell me what I can and can't do! You got that?"

Jimmy could tell she was upset. For once, he wisely decided to back off. "I'm sorry... you're right, Jules. My thing is that I just don't want to be lied to. I can't fucking take being lied to."

Maybe it finally had hit home that they were not together anymore and never would be, she thought. Hank would be their last connection to each other. She just didn't entirely trust that he would actually be cool with her seeing someone. "I don't know why you think I would lie to you. I've never, ever lied to you," she lied. "Not once."

Just then, with the worst possible timing, Tom burst into the room breathing fire. "All right, that's it! This is going to end right here, right now!" Tom screamed.

****

Hank made his way down the road back to his regular home. There was nothing particularly good to eat along the way, though there were dozens of interesting things to sniff.

He reached Julia's but heard yelling inside. He decided to hang around outside. Besides, he needed to piss and the fat lady's birdbath was looking pretty inviting.

****

"Who the fuck are you?" A surprised Jimmy asked in a tough guy tone.

"I'm her boyfriend, asshole!"

Julia closed her eyes and cussed to herself. This was the confrontation she had desperately hoped would never happen.

Jimmy turned to Julia. "I knew it! You... you... *whore!*

Tom hauled off and bitch-slapped Jimmy. "Don't call her that!"

Julia smacked Tom upside his head. "Don't you hit him."

His knee-jerk reaction was to smack her back. As soon as he did it he stood there stunned thinking first, shit, I can't believe I hit her, then, why did she hit me?

She let go of her towel to feel the sting on her face. The towel fell to the ground and she stood there naked again.

Jimmy, shocked that Tom had hit Julia, smacked Tom back. Then he noticed that Julia was naked again and just stood and stared.

"What the fuck are you looking at?" Julia screeched and smacked him. This continued on for a couple of minutes. Jimmy smacked

Julia, Tom smacked Jimmy, Julia smacked Tom, Tom smacked Julia and Jimmy smacked Tom. It was a very bizarre Three Stooges-like scene.

The last smack that Julia received caused her to stagger back and knock the trash can with her foot. She looked down and saw the condom that she had tossed the previous day when Jimmy had come to pick up Hank. She picked it up and stared at it with a confused look on her face. Tom connected with another slap to Jimmy's cheek.

"Hold it. Both of you," Julia said. She held the condom up in front of them. "It didn't come from here." Both men looked at her with bruised and bloodied faces.

"What the hell's going on? Why are you holding that?" Tom asked.

"Hank crapped out a condom and Jimmy thinks it's evidence that I'm seeing someone," Julia said.

"Well, you are," Tom said.

"Okay, sure, but what I'm saying is his evidence is bogus. This is the only one Hank could have gotten a hold of. All the others were tossed in the kitchen trash under the sink."

"Yeah, maybe," Tom said.

"What do you mean maybe?" Julia asked.

"Maybe you got a little careless with another boyfriend."

"Another boyfriend?" Jimmy and Julia shouted out in unison.

"I don't know; I'm just throwing out suggestions."

"Well stop it. You're an idiot and you're not helping."

Julia turned back to Jimmy. "Look, I'm sorry I lied. I just didn't think you could handle the truth. I never wanted to hurt you."

Jimmy's chin started to quiver. "I guess I know in my head that it's over, it's just been hard for my heart to accept."

"It's time you did," Julia said. Jimmy began to cry. She pulled him in for a hug.

Tom cleared his throat to get their attention. "Um... towel." He was not at all happy that Julia was still naked and Jimmy was shirtless. There was a lot of skin rubbing together with Jimmy's natural grease and oil acting as a lube.

Julia and Jimmy unclenched. "Oh grow up," she said. "It's not like he's never seen me naked before."

"But..."

Jimmy thought it best to fade into the background and say absolutely nothing.

"Aren't you going to be late taking your mother to bingo?" Julia said in an annoyed tone.

"She can miss the early birds, it ain't gonna kill her," Tom said.

"Just the same, why don't you leave us alone so we can talk?"

"Talk?"

"Yeah, talk, whatever."

"Whatever?"

"What are you twelve? You have to repeat everything?"

"No."

"Then go. I'll deal with you later."

Tom didn't like the sound of that.

As he walked out the front door with his head hung low he heard what sounded like a couple climaxing from sex coming from the fat lady's trailer. He was quite disgusted with the visual he got in his head. He noticed Hank sniffing around the lid-less trash cans on the side of the fat lady's. "See ya, Hank," Tom called out.

He was about to turn and leave when he saw a window slide open directly above the trash cans. A big, burly ape-hand holding a condom protruded from the window and dropped it straight down toward the intended circular target. It missed and hit the ground just inches from Hank's nose. Hank was more than delighted to sniff for a moment and then devour it. "Perfect. Just fucking perfect," Tom lamented as he turned and headed for his car.

THE RUSSIAN BRIDE

He typed the words, *All My Love, Jerry* at the bottom of the message and clicked send. Evel Kneival would hesitate to jump Jerry's smile right now – it was way too wide. He had just sent off his daily love letter e-mail to his girlfriend, the one who lived in Russia, the one he'd never met in person. If all went well in the next couple of letters he was going to ask her to marry him. He thought that on his birthday this Sunday would be perfect. It would be the ultimate present to himself.

They had met on a website called *soulmates4life.com*. Jerry subscribed to four or five dating websites but none had yielded the results that *soulmates4life.com* did. He had spent hours upon hours tweaking his profile, trying to be honest and appealing at the same time. He posted photos of himself that he thought would showcase his personality. There was the close-up one he took of himself in a suit that showed his serious, friendly, responsible side. There was one from New Years Eve 2002 taken just before he threw up in the guacamole that he hoped showed his fun side and finally, the one in the loud Hawaiian shirt taken during his vacation to Gulf Shores, Alabama that was supposed to show his easy-going side.

All that time and effort, though, had only produced a handful of responses, the most intriguing of which came from, Lena, of Kanash, Russia. He awoke one morning to find her message flashing in his e-mail in-box. Her English was far from perfect but he understood most of what she had written. According to the e-mail, Lena was a 29-year-old medical assistant who lived with her cat in a house with leaky pipes. She barely scraped by each month. She was happy for the most part even though she was unmarried when most of her friends in her village had long ago started families. Finding her soulmate would complete her, she said, as she borrowed a phrase from her favorite American movie, *Jerry Maguire.* She had decided that this would be the one and only time she would use the internet to find the love of her life so hopefully she would find Mister Right on the first try. She had carefully studied all of the available profiles and decided that Jerry was the one she would take a chance on.

Jerry found that flattering. Imagine that, a woman on the other side of the world found him interesting and attractive enough to send him an e-mail. What was wrong with those stupid Seattle women? Why couldn't they see in him what someone a half a world away could so plainly see? He wasn't the best looking guy but he certainly wasn't the worst. Sure he could lose a few pounds, but who couldn't? He had a good job in the marketing department of a major chain of coffee houses, he drove a decent car and he didn't live with his parents. In fact, he owned his own home; a nice one with a big oak tree in the backyard where he would hopefully someday hang a tire swing for his kids. What was wrong? He should have been a catch. Uglier, dumber guys than him had wives and girlfriends. He didn't understand why he couldn't find a date. He was pushing forty and was beginning to think that maybe it was just simply his destiny to be alone. Things were looking up now though, weren't they?

****

Jerry had been communicating with Lena for a month but never told anyone about it. He wanted to make sure it was real before he let anyone in on his happiness. By now he was bursting at the seams. In her last letter, Lena had professed her love for him. He was ready to tell the world.

The first opportunity he'd had to reveal his exciting news came in the form of, Les, his best friend who had joined him in line at the coffee bar in the lobby of his office building. Les, who worked in the legal department was probably the worst possible person to talk about it with. Les was a perpetual curmudgeon who had a way of ruining a person's day just by simply being around. He was a loud, rude, smarmy lawyer but for some reason Jerry thought he could count on him for some support. "Oh my God! A mail-order bride? What, are you fuckin' stupid?" Les said in a too loud voice that caused people to turn and look at them.

Jerry suddenly felt like he was standing there naked. "Shhhh. Jesus, keep your voice down," he whispered.

"Tell me you didn't fall for one of those scams. You didn't send the money yet, did you?"

"No. What money?"

"The money she'll need for her visa and plane ticket when she wants to come visit you," he said as he reached the front of the line.

"Triple large, non-fat, no foam latte. And when I say no foam it's not a suggestion it's an order. You guys completely fucked it up yesterday. In fact, I'm taking yesterday's tip back." He reached into the tip jar and took a dollar out. He shoved it in his pocket and turned back to Jerry. "The money she'll keep and never come over here."

No one except the barista saw the cashier spit into Les' cup.

"She hasn't said anything like that," Jerry said. "Just a small tea," he said to the cashier.

"Oh, she will, my naïve little friend. It'll either be that or 'the sick family member routine'. You'll see."

"You're way off base here. I think all those triple latte's are making you paranoid."

"Better to be paranoid now than sorry later," Les said as he grabbed his drink from the smirking barista. "How do you even know that she's a she?"

Jerry picked up his tea and shook his head in disgust. He was sorry he even brought it up now. "That's just stupid, okay? She sent me pictures, she's definitely not a man."

"Use your head, dude. They could be pictures of anyone. A guy could have sent you pictures of his sister and while you're sitting here jerking off to her young, nubile image, the two of them are laughing all the way to the bank," Les said.

"Not buying it. Sorry. Why do you have to be such an asshole?" Jerry said.

"Okay, don't say I didn't warn you, but just do this, okay? There are a couple of websites that keep track of this type of thing – these scammers and such; there's pictures and everything. Be smart and do some research before you do anything. Seriously, I'm telling you this as a friend."

Jerry pondered this as Les walked toward the elevator.

"Do it, man, I mean it," Les said.

Jerry hated it when Les was right.

****

After the run-in with Les, Jerry had decided not to mention Lena to anyone else. People are just plain sick, he thought. They get jealous of anyone else's happiness and trash anything that's good. Screw 'em, he thought. He wasn't going to let anyone interfere with what was supposed to be the happiest time in his life.

He spent three hours on the internet that night searching every known scammer database he could find. There were a lot of Lena's but none from Kanash. There was an <u>Alena</u> from some other city that started with a K that looked a little like her – same full lips and brown hair – but the photo was kind of fuzzy. He stared at it for a while before deciding that it definitely wasn't her. See, he thought, Les is just an idiot. Lena was for real, Jerry was sure of it. At least he was until the next morning when he opened his e-mail.

According to the e-mail, Lena's sister had been in a horrible car crash and needed emergency surgery. Her family would be able to cover most of the cost of the surgeries and the hospital stay but the medication she would need to stave off infection was beyond what they could afford. She said that asking him for money made her feel like the lowest person on earth but she had nowhere else to turn. If he could send $1,300 via Western Union she and her family would be eternally grateful. If he could not help, she would understand and still love him with all her heart. She would figure out a way to get the money. She had heard about ways a pretty Russian girl could make money doing certain things for men.

Jerry's heart sank and his head spun. If this had been yesterday morning he would have high-tailed it down to the nearest Western Union office, he might even have flown to Russia to help, but ever since Les had put the fraud bug in his ear, he didn't know what to think.

****

As soon as Jerry got to work he found Les, hauled him into his office and shut the door. "Holy shit!" Jerry yelled. "It happened just like you said. Lena said her sister had been in an accident and she needs $1,300 right away."

"What'd I tell you? I fucking knew it!" Les said, delighted to have been right. "You didn't send it yet, did you?"

Jerry paced the room like a wild man. He was clearly breaking down. "No. Help me, man. I don't know what to do."

"Okay, just calm down. Let me go downstairs and get you a Zen tea and we'll sit down and figure this thing out," Les said.

Jerry sat down and pulled up one of Lena's photos on the computer. He stared at it until Les came back with the tea and an extra large, quad shot latte for himself.

By now he had calmed down considerably. Les saw Lena's photo on the screen. "That her?"

"Yeah."

"Damn, man, that the best they got over there? I thought those Russian girls were supposed to be hot."

"Fuck you!" Jerry yelled. "If you're going to be like that you can just get out! I'll figure this out myself!"

"Oh, relax. It was a joke. She's actually pretty good-looking, I'm impressed," Les said sincerely. "You got any naked pictures of her?"

Jerry stood up from his desk and stomped toward the door.

"Okay, seriously, get out. That shit isn't funny." He stood and held the door open, waiting for Les to leave. "She's a good girl, don't talk about her like that."

Les took a seat at Jerry's desk and put his feet up. "It is funny, my friend, it's very funny, you just can't see it right now," Les said. "I say we fuck with this girl a little."

"What if she really is on the level?"

"Jesus, you're a schmuck. Look back at her letters. I'll bet you'll find that they're very general and that she rarely answers your questions."

Jerry directed Les on where to find the letters in his e-mail box. Les read them, nodded his head and smiled. Sure enough, that was the case. All the signs of a scam were right there in black and white.

Jerry slumped down in a chair and buried his head in his hands. It was finally starting to hit home. "So what do I do now?"

"Like I said, let's fuck with her," Les said with enthusiasm.

"How? What do you mean?"

"I mean, let's turn the tables on her and throw your own little personal tragedy at her. If she's for real and really loves you, she'll want to help, right?

"I guess," Jerry said.

"And if it's a scam, you'll never hear from her again. These people look for easy marks. Something gets complicated, they're gone.

"So, how do we do it?" Jerry asked.

"You just leave that to me. This is going to be fun."

****

No sooner than Les had composed and sent the message, than Jerry had second thoughts. What had seemed like a good idea at first now just seemed kind of cruel. He never should have put it in Les' hands.

The message was very emotional. He communicated concerns that she was not who she said she was and that he thought she was pulling a scam. He was emotionally fragile right now and he hoped she was for real otherwise he might have to do something drastic.

"Drastic?" Jerry asked. "What does that mean?"

"I thought you were going to let me handle this," Les said.

"I am, I just don't want you to fuck this up in case she's not a fraud."

"Remind me again how much experience you have with women."

"Fine, you handle it."

"That's what I thought. Let me know when the response comes in."

****

The response was flashing in the in-box the next morning. Jerry did not want to see what Lena had to say. He was scared to death, in fact. He waited painfully until he got to the office. He wanted Les to open it and prepare him for the results.

Les read the note. If tears could come through e-mail, surely there would be a flood in Jerry's office. At least that was Jerry's perspective. Les had his doubts. "Smells like bullshit to me," he said. "This girl is way too emotional to be for real. You guys haven't even met for Christ sake."

"It doesn't matter when you're as in love as we are," Jerry said.

Les shot him a look of disgust. "We'll just see about that." He began to type.

"What are you doing?" Jerry asked.

"You'll see."

Jerry tried to get a look at what Les was typing. Les held him off with one hand and kept typing with the other. "Putting the final nail in this coffin once and for all," Les said, clearly having fun.

"Don't! Just forget it! I don't want to do this anymore!" Jerry begged.

Les clicked send and it was done.

"Asshole!"

"You're better off. We'll find you a nice local girl," Les said smugly.

"I don't want a nice local girl, I want Lena. Now I gotta figure out how to fix this."

Les stood and headed for the door. His job was done. "Leave it alone, my friend. Fate has intervened."

And then Les was gone. Jerry sat down and buried his head in his hands for a moment. He wondered how and why he had become friends with that asshole. He took a deep breath. The how's and why's didn't matter now, he was done with Les. There was no way he could be friends with someone who had so little respect for his feelings; someone who could so heartlessly sabotage someone else's happiness. Even with the doubt as to Lena's sincerity, there was no call for what he had done.

Jerry took a deep breath and looked up at the screen. He pulled up his sent mail box and read what Les had written.

> *Lena,*
>
> *I loved you with all my heart but all you could do was so cruelly rip it out and stomp on it. You have destroyed me with your lies. I'm sure my death will not faze you in the least. I would rather die than suffer the humiliation you have caused me. I was going to ask you to marry me this Sunday, my birthday. It shall now also be the day I died.*
>
> *See you in Hell!*
> *Jerry*

"Holy Shit!" Jerry said out loud. "That sick son of a bitch!"

He clicked on compose and wrote a desperate message explaining how it had been someone else who had written the last message and that everything was just a horrible prank played by a horrible man. He was not going to kill himself. He just wanted things to get back to normal. He typed his usual, All My Love, Jerry at the bottom of the message and clicked send. And then he waited. He sat and stared at the computer screen waiting for a response.

He had forgotten that it was eleven hours later in her part of Russia. She had told him that she only had access to a computer at work and since it was well into the evening in Russia she surely would have gone home by now. Plus it was Friday night over there, he probably wouldn't get anything until Monday. Those thoughts never crossed his mind, though and he got absolutely nothing done all day.

He left work early, went home and booted up his computer. All that was in his in-box was several spams that all promised to enhance his sex life. There was nothing from Lena, the love of his life. He pulled out the envelope that contained the lock of hair she had sent him. He smelled it and rubbed it between his fingers. He cried for a moment but then tried to think about his next move. He somehow needed to get proactive.

Jerry thought maybe his e-mail delivery system might be faulty so he set up new accounts with six different e-mail providers and sent Lena the same exact message through each one of them. The rest of the night was spent surfing from one e-mail account to the next. He spent some time on travel sites looking for flights to Moscow, but as he researched it, he realized he didn't have the necessary paperwork in order to make the trip. He was going to have to wait until she got in touch with him and the waiting was driving him insane.

He woke to the sound of rain pounding on his windows. It was daytime now. He looked around; the chair had been his bed. He wasn't sure when he had drifted off but he estimated it was around 3 AM. He went through the ritual of checking all his e-mail boxes but found nothing but spam. Now he knew for certain that something was wrong. All of Lena's past e-mails had been received between midnight and 6 AM, five days a week without fail. A look at the clock on the wall showed it was way past 7. This was bad. Jerry was experiencing a slow burn. With each passing moment and no response from Lena, his thoughts became more and more violent. He was going to kill that motherfucker, Les and he didn't care if he went to jail, it would so be worth it.

It continued like that for hours. If Jerry had to leave the room for any reason - to piss or whatever - he would come right back and go through the checking ritual again. About noon he started throwing things around. He broke anything and everything of value, except his computer. By five there was nothing left to break, he had completely trashed his home. There was only one other thing left untouched – the bottle of expensive Russian Vodka he had bought to celebrate her visit, whenever that was going to be.

Jerry stared at the bottle for a few moments then sat down and checked his e-mail again. Still nothing. He cracked open the bottle and took a hefty swig. Since he had taken his eyes off the screen to take a drink, he had to go through the checking ritual again to make sure he hadn't missed anything. This went on for about an hour until he had drunk half the bottle.

Just after six he passed out in his chair. He remained there until 7:30 when he regained just enough consciousness to realize he was going to puke. With his eyes barely open, he stumbled his way toward the bathroom. He tripped over some books that he had thrown from the bookshelf that that was now in a hundred pieces in the hallway. He fell to the floor, short of his destination and threw up uncontrollably all over the hardwood floor. He passed out again with his face in the puddle of barf. He didn't move again until Sunday afternoon, some twenty hours later.

Jerry never heard the knocks at his door around 11 PM. He never saw Lena's pretty face in his window as she rapped desperately on the glass. He never heard her scream his name when she saw him lying on the floor not moving or responding. If there were any doubts she was for real, they most assuredly would have been gone by now.

Lena had been so worried about the man she had loved but never met that she left her sister's side, pilfered money from her family – money needed for her sister's medical care – and caught the first flight to America. Her sister would later lose both of her legs to infection.

After an angst-filled eighteen-hour flight, she had arrived at Jerry's home in Seattle ready to do whatever it took to save him from suicide. The sight of him face down on floor, unresponsive, told her it was too late. She threw a fit and banged her hands bloody on his door. The sound of the heavy rain muffled her shrieks from his neighbors. She dropped to her knees, buried her head in her hands and bawled until every last ounce of energy was used up.

****

The next morning, Jerry stood in his den looking and smelling like complete shit. He could not believe he had gone so crazy. It had been a hell of a weekend. His head was pounding; he had the worst hangover ever. He had spent most of his birthday passed out in puke. He knew there was no way he could handle the usual Monday morning bullshit at work so he called in sick. He stared for a moment at his computer that had long ago gone into hibernation mode. He knew deep down that there would be no message from Lena, but he wanted to check anyway. The computer booted up and he realized he was right. There would be no tantrum this time, only quiet resignation. He shut off the computer and headed for the shower. He hoped that would make him feel better.

It wasn't until he stepped out of the shower and opened the window to let the steam out that he saw her. For a second he thought he was seeing things but quickly realized he wasn't. He began to panic and hyperventilate. He scrambled out to his backyard.

Lena, in her despondence over Jerry's apparent suicide, went into his backyard, found an extension cord in his patio and used it to hang herself from his oak tree. He pulled her down and did what he could to try to revive her. He cradled her stiff body in his arms and yelled for help over and over. It was hopeless. She had long since died, brokenhearted and alone in the pouring rain.

THE TRUTH ABOUT THE CHAIR

Let me get this out of the way right away: I've been told I can sometimes have a bit of an anger problem. Until recently, I didn't think of it as that big of a deal - I get mad, I break something, I'm over it. No problem. Sometimes it's not too good when it happens in a public place like the grocery store or a cross-country flight. Trust me, I know. But what can I say; people just get under my skin. The other night there was an incident at work that made me open my eyes and see that maybe I needed to calm down, step back and take a look at myself. Usually, right after I break something, if it affected someone else, I would make up some bullshit story to cover. It seemed to be an effective option until the night before last when it all came crashing down - literally.

I work for a New York City-based music video channel that's beamed into more than 40 million homes in North America. My job is to sit and watch the videos, commercials and promos and make sure everything plays in order, on time and without technical glitches. I work a 12-hour overnight shift in a windowless room by myself. It's the perfect job for someone who dislikes being around people.

Two nights ago, I don't know what it was, but managers from several different departments - sales, promotions and scheduling - kept calling me with asinine requests to change the schedule, dub this, copy that. They were really pissing me off. After the idiot promotions manager called at two in the morning with her fourth replacement request of the night, I lost it and slammed my chair to the floor. Childish, yes, but it made me feel a whole hell of a lot better - until I went to pick up the chair. I realized that the back had detached from the seat. The cheap-ass piece of plastic that held the back to the seat snapped clean in half.

Lately I had broken quite a few items. Some tapes, a phone and my boss' ten-year anniversary personalized coffee cup with the company logo on it were all victims of my rage. I worried that destroying a $300 office chair just might be the thing that sent me packing. My boss, Gary, is a good guy who puts up with way too much of my shit. I am a relentless smartass but he always defends me whenever one of our sleazy salespeople or an idiot promotions person get all bent out of shape by one of my not-so-subtle insults toward them. The truth is, he doesn't like those people either so I think he has a secret admiration for my blunt style.

The next night, Gary was waiting to talk to me. Usually, he is on his way home to Staten Island long before I get in at seven. I knew this wasn't going to be good.

"Hey, Gary, what's keeping you around so late?" I asked, knowing full well.

"Apparently we need to have a little conversation about taking care of our tools around here," he said.

"Well personally, I wash mine in the shower every day and whenever I can, I try to slip it into a nice, tight box..."

"That's funny. I think you know what I'm talking about."

"Well if you're not talking about our dicks, you must be talking about the chair. Look, it was just like I said in my e-mail, I was leaning back and the fucker just snapped."

"Yeah, so you said. Frankly, I'm a little shocked, you actually came up with something that almost sounds reasonable this time."

"What did you expect?" I said. "You want to hear something like 'gee, Gary, I was fucking some fat chick on the chair and it just fell apart?'"

"Actually, that's more like it. That's so much more creative and entertaining," Gary said.

"I wish that's the way it went."

"Yeah, well as good as 'it just snapped' sounds, I'm not really buying it. I think just once I'd like to hear the truth."

"You have a better version?"

"How about something like, 'gee, Gary, I got pissed at the promotions department and threw the fucker to the floor?'"

"I don't really like that one," I said. "Entertaining? Maybe. Creative? Definitely not."

Gary shook his head in disbelief then looked at his watch. "I have to go but let me leave you with this little thought. The general manager is not real happy with you right now. He told me to tell you that if you so much as break a pencil lead, you're out of here."

"Uh oh, I pissed off the man upstairs."

Gary slipped his coat on, picked up his satchel and headed for the door. "This is no joke. I won't be able to help you next time. I think maybe you should get some help with the anger thing."

I could see the seriousness in his eyes and hear it in his tone. I got serious too. "Don't worry, things will be fine," I said. "Thanks, Gary."

"Remember what I said. Be careful. And don't break anything."

****

I thought about it all night. I really did need to calm down. This was a good job that paid well for doing almost nothing. It would be really stupid to get fired because I can't control my anger. I looked at the clock, it was almost eleven. I was jonesing for a smoke.

I walked down a flight of stairs, out the non-descript metal door and onto West 58th Street. I stuck my foot between the door and the frame so it wouldn't close and lock. I fished out a smoke and my zippo out of my jeans and lit another 3-inch pleasure stick. I took a long, satisfying drag and turned to stare into the security camera perched above the door. I smugly blew smoke up toward the lens then turned and took a look down the street. Not too busy, only a handful of people out. I looked up the street in the other direction. The view was much better. Two girls that looked to be in their early 20's were heading my way.

The blonde one was about 5'5, average weight and a decent set of tits. Her red mini-skirt revealed a killer pair of legs. I could easily imagine them wrapped around my neck. As she got closer though, I could see that if I had to look at that face while I was doing her, I would have nightmares for months. With her, it would have to be doggy-style.

Her brunette friend was interesting. She was about the same height but looked to be packing a huge ass and a pair of giant knockers. Her jeans were so tight I could almost hear the seams cry out in pain. As she got closer, I could see she was absolutely stunning. How ironic that the one that you'd want to do from behind because of her great, huge bubble ass was also the one you wouldn't mind actually looking in the eyes. Go figure.

I noticed that they both had unlit cigarettes between their fingers. "Oh, let's ask this guy," I heard the blonde say. "Hey, you got a light?"

"Yeah. Here," I said. I whipped out the zippo and did this thing I'd been practicing where with one snap of my fingers, the lid snaps back and the lighter comes to life.

They glanced at each other and smirked. "What, you got magic fingers or something?" the blonde asked sarcastically.

"You want the light or what?" I asked, annoyed. Damn she was homely.

"Yeah," she said. They both put their cigarettes to their lips and leaned in toward the flame.

The brunette pulled back, took a puff and pointed at my head. "You work for them?"

I pulled my baseball cap off and looked at front of it. I realized I was wearing one that had the channel's logo on it. "Yep."

"That's cool, I love that channel, I watch it all the time."

That's probably how her ass got so big, I thought to myself. Not that there's anything wrong with that.

"Me too," said the blonde. "What do you do?" Watching TV didn't explain how this one got to be butt-ugly.

"I work in the control room, playing the videos and pushing buttons and shit," I said, downplaying to a couple of obvious fans.

"That's a cool job. I always wondered who did that kind of stuff." The brunette said as she stuck out her hand. "I'm Rita, this is Vicki."

I shook their hands and chatted them up for a few minutes until we had all smoked our cigarettes down to the filters. Rita seemed to be very interested in my job so I decided to invite them up for a tour.

I showed them the studios, the edit bays, the dressing rooms and the control room where I worked. Every chance I got I glanced at various parts of Rita - tits, ass, camel toe - whatever I could. At one point she bent over to tie her shoe and I got a good look at her black lace thong. She was really turning me on. I think she knew it too. A connection was in the works.

Vicki seemed bored. "We should go, our friends are probably wondering where we are."

Rita looked at her watch and sadly agreed. I got the feeling she would rather stay. I hoped it was more than her just being excited to be inside the bowels of her favorite channel. Nevertheless, I walked them down to the street, lit up a smoke and said goodbye. I watched them walk down the street and disappear around the corner onto Broadway. Too bad, I thought. I crushed out the cigarette and went back to work.

****

In my dream there was a buzzer. I awoke suddenly. I was disoriented for a moment but as I came to my senses, I realized I had fallen asleep at work. I wasn't going to hang onto my job by doing that shit. Luckily, we were still on the air and everything appeared to be playing fine. Thank God for automation. The last time I remember looking at the clock it was 1:15. It was now 2:40. Out for over an hour. How pathetic. The buzzer went off again. It was the doorbell. It was then that I realized that it was that buzzer that had jarred me from sleep in the first place. I looked up at the security monitor and sprang to my feet when I saw Rita standing there waving into the camera.

I bounded down the stairs and opened the door. "Hey, what are you doing here? Where's your friend?"

"After hours club. I was bored; they were mostly her friends from work anyway. I thought you might like some company. Is that allowed?"

"Yeah, I guess - for a bit anyway. Come on in."

****

As it turned out, Rita was somewhat of a video expert. We spent quite a while sitting at my console looking through the database and pulling up old, obscure videos to watch on a studio monitor. Some of the videos probably hadn't been viewed since the '80's. We were getting along very well and seemed to have a lot in common. It was a good time.

After about an hour, Rita excused herself to the restroom and I took another opportunity to check out her ass. While she was gone I actually did some of what I was getting paid to do. I didn't have a lot of duties but I had managed to fall behind in the ones I did have.

I didn't hear her come back into the room. She snuck up behind me, wrapped her arms around me and began to nibble on my ear. I was pleasantly surprised. I let her nibble for a second then spun my chair around and kissed her. She jammed her tongue so far down my throat I was afraid she'd rupture my esophagus. I slid a hand up her shirt, slipped it into her bra and grabbed a handful of soft flesh. It was wonderfully natural. She didn't seem to mind so I did the same with my other hand.

She let out a quick grunt. I wasn't sure whether it was pleasure or pain. She withdrew her tongue from the depths of my solar plexus and looked me straight in the eyes. Shit, I fucked up, I thought. A sly grin appeared on her face. She got down on her knees and repositioned herself between my legs. I was so hard it was starting to hurt.

She unbuckled my belt and unzipped my jeans. She grabbed the top of them and slid them down my hips. I pushed up in the chair to make it a little easier, but my dick got pinched in the process anyway. I let out a grunt of my own - and not one of pleasure. She looked up at me. I faked a smile through the pain then took control of the situation by taking them down the rest of the way.

Rita was delighted when my dick popped out. The pain quickly subsided. I think my dick was delighted to be out too. What a trooper. She took hold of my cock, stroked it a few times and looked up at me with seductive eyes I haven't seen since that whore blew me at my buddy's bachelor party down in Atlantic City.

She started licking the head like a lollipop and for a brief moment I remembered an old TV commercial where this cartoon owl was trying to determine the number of licks it took to get to the tootsie roll center of a tootsie-pop. "Ah one... ah two... ah three..." he'd say before biting the thing in half and declaring the number to be three. I shuddered. She must've thought it was because of her because she looked up, smiled then swallowed me whole.

The heat in her mouth was incredible. Her lips slowly moved up and down the shaft. I knew I wouldn't last long. I tried to think of something else, anything else to keep it going longer. Snap, Crackle and Pop, the three little guys from the Rice Krispies commercials popped into my head. Why was I thinking about cartoon characters while getting a blowjob? I didn't get it. My thoughts drifted from there to Rice Krispie treats. Oh, how I love those. And finally to the time my mother made them with Fruity Pebbles. You want to taste a little piece of heaven, try that sometime. My mom sure had some good ideas. Mom? Now I was thinking of mom while getting blown? Jesus Christ! That's just fucking disturbing!

She suddenly stopped and stood up. It was as if she knew what I was thinking about. She began to unfasten her jeans. Okay, that works. She jammed her thumbs between the waistband and her hips and tried to wriggle out of her jeans. No one told her you can't wriggle free of paint. Those jeans were not coming off easily. I stuck my thumbs in there to help. I was going to get me some of that no matter what. Good Christ those jeans were tight.

I put some ooommff into it and the jeans came down, black thong and all. I could have sworn I heard the seams of her jeans whisper "thank you". Or maybe it was my cock saying "thank you", because I was now staring directly at her perfect, bare pussy. Not a hair, goose bump or pimple to be found. She stepped between my legs, leaned forward and stuck her tongue down my throat again. I clumsily felt around her pussy lips until I found the hole. She was already so wet and hot, I thought I could probably skip all the foreplay and get right to the good stuff.

Rita must have been reading my mind because she lifted a leg and swung it over mine. My finger slipped out. She was now straddling my knee. She swung her other leg over my other leg. My cock was now standing straight up and resting against her slit. I closed my eyes as she stood on her tiptoes, grabbed the shaft of my cock and positioned it at the opening of her pussy. I could already feel the heat on the tip of my dick.

It was then that I felt something from somewhere within the structure of the chair snap. My eyes popped open and I froze, waiting. Please God, don't do this, my thoughts begged. She lowered down and took all of me in. Snap number two sounded like a clap of lightning. I looked up at her face. Her eyes were closed. She apparently was unaffected by the sounds. She slowly rose up. "No wait!" I screamed. It was too late. She was already coming back down for stroke number two when the chair didn't just fall apart – it disintegrated!

We fell hard to the floor, pieces of the chair scattered across the room. I was on my back and she was on top of me. Miraculously, I was still inside her. She burst out laughing like it was the funniest fucking thing she'd ever seen. I was in shock. All I could do was look around the room in horror. There couldn't be more debris if Godzilla had come to town.

Rita was having a great time. She couldn't stop laughing. It was starting to piss me off. "Stop it! It's not funny!"

She couldn't catch her breath. I shoved her off of me. She laughed on.

"I said it's not funny! I am so fucking fired!" I scrambled to my feet and pulled my pants up.

Her laughter began to subside when she saw how pissed I was. "What's the big deal? It's just a chair."

"You don't understand, I break shit around here all the time. The man upstairs said I'd be gone if I broke one more thing."

"Since when does God care if you break a chair?"

"Not *that* man upstairs," I said. I pointed toward the staircase across the room. "The general manager! The man! Upstairs!"

"Oh," she said, sitting there amid the disaster, somehow not looking so sexy anymore.

I was manic. How could I have been so stupid? "You gotta go," I said, as I grabbed her arm to help her up.

"Are you serious? Why?"

"Why? Because you do, that's why. I need to figure this out."

I scooped up her jeans and thong, handed them to her and rushed her toward the stairs.

"Hey!" she screamed. "Hold on, I'm not dressed!"

"Hurry up then," I said, pushing her naked ass closer to the exit.

"Okay, okay, Jesus!"

She pulled her jeans on but was facing the near-impossible task of buttoning them. I had no patience for that. "Close enough," I said, pulling her down the stairs. I was kind of forceful, it's a wonder she didn't trip and fall.

By the time I knocked open the door and pushed her out onto the sidewalk, the jeans were barely on. She worked frantically to button them. "I'll call you," I said as I pulled the door shut behind me. I could have sworn I heard her call me a fucking asshole as I bounded back up the stairs, but I can't be sure.

I stood there looking at the mess, ready to cry. I had no idea how I was going to explain it. I had finally done it. I was fucked.

****

I didn't get a wink of sleep that morning. I laid there and waited for my cell phone to light up with Gary's number. I had sent him an e-mail that I hoped he would get before the morning shift had a chance to tell him that I had destroyed the new chair. I didn't see any way I was going to save my job. Gary would never believe the truth. That particular truth would get me fired anyway. I decided to tell him what he'd been wanting to hear: that I got pissed off and destroyed the chair. I figured if I actually admitted to an anger problem and promised to seek help, they might let me keep my job conditionally.

Oddly enough, the call never came. I was going to have to go in to work and face the music. Why couldn't Gary just fire me over the phone like they did at my two previous jobs? Maybe my plan had worked. It was the longest day of my life.

****

As I suspected, Gary was waiting for me when I got in. "Close the door and sit down," he said, as I entered his office.

"I know what you're going to say. Give me 5 minutes to pack up my shit and I'll get out of your hair."

"Relax," he said, "I just want you to tell me the truth, that's all."

"Didn't you read your e-mail?"

"I did. That wasn't the truth."

"Yes it was. Like I said, I got pissed and destroyed the chair."

Gary shook his head in disbelief. "Watch this," he said, as he pushed play on the VCR on his desk.

There on the screen was the surveillance tape from the camera over the door. The video was of me escorting Rita out of the building and of her struggling to fasten her jeans on the street just outside the door. "You actually did fuck a fat chick up here didn't you?" he asked.

I was horrified. I was so caught. "She wasn't really fat, she just had this great, huge ass and great big titties," I said, not knowing what else to say.

He shut off the VCR and leaned back in his chair with a shit-eating grin on his face. "You crazy sonofabitch," he said.

"Huh."

"A similar thing happened to me 15 years ago at this shitty affiliate down in Pittsburgh, only my little encounter actually knocked us off the air."

"No shit?"

"No shit. I was fucking this chick in a chair. She had this beautiful, long black hair that was unbelievably soft. Anyway, we were going at it hot and heavy while I was airing an episode of Star Trek when suddenly she swings around and gets her hair caught in the on-air reel to reel machine. Hosed up the fucking thing like you wouldn't believe. I had dead air for five minutes. I didn't know whether to try to get her unstuck or solve my dead air problem.

"What did you do?" I asked.

"What else? I worked on the dead air problem."

I couldn't help but laugh at that little scenario.

"It's funny now, but I got my ass bounced out of there the next day," he said.

"Is that what's happening here? Am I getting my ass bounced out of here?"

"Under the circumstances, I'm feeling kind of sympathetic. If you'll pay for a new chair, I think I can keep a lid on this one."

I breathed a huge sigh of relief. "Thanks, Gary, I don't know what to say."

"That doesn't mean that the next time you get mad and break something, that I won't can your ass."

"I know, I'm going to get help."

"I hope so. Now get the hell out of here and get to work."

****

So, it's only been one day, but I'm feeling confident that I won't lose my temper at work anymore. I was faced with the prospect of losing the best job I ever had and I really don't want to do that. I feel bad about the way things ended with Rita. I was a total asshole. Maybe if I'm lucky I'll get the chance to see her again. Whatever happens, believe me, there will be no more lies and no more smashing things. And the next time, I definitely won't fuck anyone in a chair.

THE ROCK STAR

There isn't really any other way to put it so I'll just go ahead and be blunt: rock stars make my pussy wet. It gets so wet I had to stop wearing panties to concerts altogether. Not that I needed them anyway, I pretty much always lost them. I just can't stand the feeling of soaked cloth between my legs.

Back in the 80's my pussy was wet constantly due to the high number of glam-rock, hair bands out there. Even standing in line to buy concert tickets would get my juices flowing. There was something about the wild, flowing hair, the tattoos, the earrings and the spandex that made me lose control.

I fucked my first rock star on Halloween night in 1986. He was only the bass player, but still, he was in a huge band, so for me, that was good enough. I was dressed like a total slut. What I wore barely qualified as a costume much less clothing; it was really just a skimpy leotard, fishnets and some cat ears. I was sixteen and he was the first of thousands.

The Rock Star

In order to get to the bands, I had to do a lot of "favors" for roadies and tour managers. I sampled so much salami I could have opened a deli. Some of the guys were cute, so it wasn't too bad, but for the most part it was just about moving on to the next level. I've heard guys make all kinds of references to stinky fish when talking about the smell of pussy but I have to tell you, a sweaty stick of lap taffy in a sweltering backstage broom closet doesn't smell too much fucking different.

I struggled through six aimless years of community college and finally dropped out eighteen credits shy of that damned, elusive Associates degree (my concert habit made it hard to study.) The town I live in, Fairfield, California, is situated along Interstate 80 halfway between San Francisco and Sacramento. Since Fairfield is less than an hour drive away from both of those cities, there always seemed to be a concert happening. I was able to convince the local newspaper, *The Daily Republic*, that they needed someone to do concert reviews and interviews on a freelance basis. If they liked the article, they'd buy it, if they didn't, fuck it, I got to go to the concert for free. At first I didn't really care about the articles; I just wanted the backstage press credentials so I could quit blowing roadies for access. As it turned out, I actually had natural talent as a writer and journalist. The paper liked my work and my unapologetically blunt style so they ended up buying every article.

After twelve years of sex with rock stars and four years of writing about them, I was satisfied with my life. I had even learned to take journalism and the craft of writing seriously and as a result I made a decent living with the newspaper and even sold some articles to the big music magazines as well. But best of all, I still got good, stiff dick every time a band came anywhere near northern California.

As the 80's moved into the 90's, glam rock gave way to the grunge movement and I went right along with it. The grunge rockers were more cerebral and disturbed. The glam rockers would get everyone high, fuck your brains out then pass out on the bed. The grunge rockers would want to make love and then kick you out so they could get high by themselves and pass out on the floor.

Around the late 90's, after having been more or less out of the picture for almost a decade, the hair bands began to make a comeback, much to my delight. While I had gotten used to flannel shirts, ripped jeans and oily hair, I really missed the old days. As each reunited band trickled back through town, I renewed my old acquaintances.

While I was excited that my old conquests were starting to come around again, there was one in particular that excited me more than most. The band was called Beavertrap and the lead singer was a mountain of a man named Randy Dodd. At 6'5, 280 lbs, long, wavy, black hair and two full sleeves of tattoos, he was quite the fabulous, intimidating specimen.

Randy was my all-time favorite singer and the only one who I never had sex with. My pussy got wet just thinking about him. But now he was coming back to town and I was determined to have his tree-trunk cock inside me one way or another.

I was not yet writing for the paper the last time Beavertrap had come to town and it was one of those rare instances where I had sucked off the roadie only to still be denied backstage access. Randy was the missing trophy in my case.

Legend had it that he was so temperamental that he could snap and turn on an interviewer instantly if he didn't like where the line of questioning was headed. He quit talking to the media altogether back in '89 when an interview with a guy from *Rolling Stone* went awry.

The guy lost a couple of teeth while Randy lost $2.5 million in the civil suit that followed. Finally Randy had decided that enough time had gone by and enough hours had been spent on anger management that he would resume talking with the media. This album and tour was a comeback of sorts and at this juncture of their career, Beavertrap needed all the publicity they could get.

We were set to meet at 2 p.m. in his suite at the Four Seasons Hotel in San Francisco. Perfect, I thought. I'd rather fuck in a bed than a Starbucks restroom or a tour bus bunk. I spent the morning doing maintenance and research. I wanted to find out if he had any pussy preferences. I would hate to finally get my chance to screw Randy's brains out and show up with my natural, full bush only to find out he preferred it bare. I could not afford a faux pas of that nature.

I dug out Beavertrap's tell-all book but strangely, I couldn't find any references to his preferences. I could have sworn there were whole chapters devoted to their sex-capades in their book. No wait, that was Motley Crue. Anyway, I decided to play it safe and shave it all off. Easy come, easy go, right? It'll itch like hell growing back, but that's a small price to pay. I douched twice, again, to play it safe. The more I thought about it though, I couldn't figure out why, with all the research I had done, I could find absolutely no accounts of sexual activity by Randy with anyone. Everybody knew he had never been married but there was also no mention anywhere about girlfriends or otherwise. Every rock band autobiography out there included sex stories - every one except Randy's. I guess he was a little more reclusive than I thought.

I dug out a black chiffon blouse and my shortest spandex mini. I put on my favorite black bra - one that made my 36 C's look fucking amazing. I thought fishnets would be a little over the top so I chose simple black stockings, a garter belt and my favorite four-inch fuck-me pumps. Of course there was no way I was wearing panties. I was already starting to feel moist down there. I stared at myself in the mirror. Damn, I looked hot. If I were a guy, I would so want to fuck the shit out of me. In fact, if I were a lesbian, I think I'd want to fuck the shit out of me too.

I knocked on Randy's door precisely at two. He answered promptly and I was totally awestruck. He towered over my tight 5'5 frame and even though he smiled kindly down at me, I was still intimidated.

"Sara, right?" he asked.

"Yes," is all I could say.

Please come in," he said as he kissed my hand.

All he'd done was utter my name and I could already feel the moisture between my legs. He led me over to the sectional sofa. His ass was absolutely sublime in the tight leather pants he was wearing. The black Harley Davidson wife-beater allowed me a view of his hard-as-rock arms. I could not wait until he would use them to pin my legs behind my head.

"Please, sit down," he said. He was a perfect gentleman and he seemed quite relaxed compared to the wild man he is on stage.

As I sat down I briefly wondered if I should give him a beaver shot right away or wait a bit. I decided on a ladylike approach and wait a bit.

"Would you like something to drink? I apologize but I only have juice and bottled water."

"Water would be fine, thank you," I said, anxious to ditch the small talk and get down to what I came here for.

"Before we get started, I just want to make it clear that I'll only be talking about the new album and the tour," he said. "Everything else is either in the Beavertrap book or been discussed ad nauseum in articles over the years. I have no desire to revisit the past."

He handed me a bottle of Fiji water and sat down on the sofa across from me. He crossed his long legs and settled in for some conversation.

"Actually, I have a different slant I'd like to explore," I said.

"Fine, as long as your article is about *this* album and *this* tour." He started to look a little less relaxed.

"I don't really give a fuck about the article," I said in my usual blunt, get-right-to-the-point style.

He stood up and looked annoyed. If I thought he was intimidating before, it was nothing compared to the way he looked down at me while I remained sitting. I have to admit, it was a little scary. "Well then, if there's nothing to talk about I guess you'll be going," he said, extending his hand.

I decided to hold my ground. "Sit down, Randy, I'm just getting started."

"Excuse me?" he said, as shocked as I was that had come out of my mouth.

"I'm not going anywhere until I get what I came for."

"Oh really? And what might that be?"

"Sit down and I'll explain it to you, my neck is starting to hurt from looking up at you like this."

He kind of grunted but went ahead and sat down anyway. He must have been intrigued otherwise he might have tried to throw me out. I'm sure people don't usually talk to him like that but I learned a long time ago that you never get what you want if you're not assertive – even from horny rock stars.

I stood up, walked across the top of the coffee table that separated us then stepped down in front of him. It was his turn to crane his neck up at me. "I came here for sex, pure and simple," I said. "If I get an article out of it, so be it." I slowly hiked my skirt up to my waist and revealed to him my freshly shaved bare snatch.

He stared at it for a second then looked up at me. He looked a bit angry. "You want to get that thing out of my face, please?" he said.

I rubbed my fingers across my pussy lips then spread them to give him a clear view of my wet, swollen clit. "How about you bury your face in here instead?"

"I don't think so," he said, with his teeth clenched and his anger growing. "Pull your skirt down before you cause yourself any more embarrassment."

"I'm not embarrassed."

"You should be. Now get out of my face before you're sorry you came here."

It was a clear threat but I'd waited too long for this opportunity and I did not believe he was going make good on it. "Don't threaten me, Randy. Be a good boy and do what I tell you." I crawled onto his lap and straddled him.

He put his hands around my waist. I knew he'd cave. There isn't a man alive who is going pass this up. Instead, I found myself flying through the air. I landed on my back a few feet away on another part of the sectional. That is how strong this guy was. From his sitting position he had lifted all 117 pounds of me over his head and tossed me away like a rag doll.

He got up and stood over me. At first I thought he was finally going to give me what I wanted but then I saw the anger on his face and I realized I could be in a bit of trouble. "Get up and get out!" he yelled.

Now I was pissed. Who the hell did he think he was turning me down like that? "What are you a faggot?" I blurted out. "You a little gay boy?" When I thought about my outburst much later, I was sorry I had used those terms in that way, but in the heat of the moment, that's what came out.

"No wonder I couldn't find any info on your sex life, you've been hiding the fact that you like to take it up the poop chute. Wait until the world gets a hold of that little nugget."

He grabbed me under an armpit and pulled me off the sofa. My ass hit the floor hard. "Hey, Goddammit!" I screamed. I looked up and saw he had a strange look on his face that wasn't quite fear and wasn't quite remorse. I thought maybe he was afraid I would sue him for another 2.5 mil for manhandling me.

He stuck out his hand, presumably to help me up. "It wasn't supposed to go like that," he said. "You're supposed to stand when someone takes you by the arm like that."

"That's a poor excuse for an apology."

"It wasn't an apology, only an explanation. Oh and by the way, I'm not gay."

I realized my skirt was still hiked up around my waist and I was flat on my back with my legs spread. That might have been my original goal, or some version of it, but now I was feeling angry, embarrassed and decidedly not sexy. I swatted his hand away, pulled myself up off the floor and adjusted my skirt to cover up the goods.

"Whatever. Maybe you're gay, maybe you have some kind of fucked up STD, it doesn't matter, once you put your hands on me in that way I stopped giving a shit."

I stomped toward the door. He jumped in front of me and blocked my exit. "Oh no you don't. You're not leaving here until I know what you're going to write about me."

I stuck my finger hard into his chest. "You know what? I can pretty much write any fucking thing I want and there isn't a fucking thing you can do about it."

"Oh really."

"That's right. With as much trouble you've been in over the years, you've got no credibility. The public knows you to be hot-headed and short-tempered and any other hyphenate I can throw in there. If it comes down to your word against mine, who do you think they're going to believe: A respected journalist or the oft-sued rock star with a penchant for violence?"

"Is that a threat?"

"You bet your ass it is. Now get the fuck out of my way before I throw attempted rape into the mix."

I pushed my way past him and made it to the door. I honestly did not know what I would write; I just knew that no good could come once the threats started flying. I don't know if he took mine seriously or not but I did not want to wait around to find out. Normally, nothing scares me, but I have to tell you, at that moment I was quaking in my four-inch fuck-me heels.

I barely got the door open before he came up behind me and slammed it shut. I was trapped between him and the door. I could feel his warm breath on my neck. Any other time that might make me hot but at that moment I was frozen in fear. I couldn't even scream.

"Please don't leave," he said.

The anger in his voice seemed to be gone but I thought that made him even scarier and unpredictable. I felt the first tear roll down my cheek.

"I'm not going to hurt you but I want to show you something. If I let you go will you stay a moment?"

I really just wanted to make a run for it. I told him I would stay even though I honestly didn't know if I would.

"You need to back way off."

"Whatever you want," he said. He let go of me and did what I asked. I turned around and looked at him but kept one hand on the door handle.

"I've wanted to be a rock star ever since I was a little kid," he began. "When I was about seven I stumbled across *The Monkees* TV show. I had always listened to the radio and loved music, but once I actually saw a band perform with instruments, even though I found out later that they weren't really playing, I was instantly hooked. From that moment on I watched anything that had to do with music; *American Bandstand* on Saturday mornings, *Don Kirshner's Rock Concert* on Saturday nights and anything else I could find."

"Those shows always had throngs of screaming women clamoring for attention from the band. That didn't mean a thing to me until I was about ten or eleven when I finally started to notice girls. I suddenly realized the power rock stars have with the opposite sex; they can have sex with any woman they want, whenever they want. That's what I wanted."

"And that's what you got. Where are you going with this?"

"You assume that's what I got. Do you believe in God, Sara?"

"Not really but I have to say there's been many a morning where I've done my share of praying."

"Well let me tell you from experience that if there is a God, he has one hell of a cruel sense of humor. Would you believe that I have only had sex twice in my entire life?"

"Not for a Goddamn second."

"It's absolutely true and you want to know why?"

"I'm not sure," I said. For some reason I was no longer scared that I would be the victim of a violent outburst. He had suddenly taken on a boyish, less masculine, less threatening personality. I still couldn't help but wonder if what he was saying were true, why this magnificent specimen of a man had only sex twice in his life. It had to be bullshit. Then it hit me. Holy shit! Maybe he's really a woman!

Before I realized what was happening he had undone his belt and was unzipping his tight leather pants. "Uh what the fuck are you doing?"

"You need to see to understand," he said as he pulled them down to his knees.

I gasped in shock. I instantly understood. Okay, definitely not a woman, but what the fuck? All I could see was pubic hair and a head. His dick looked like a tiny little pink mushroom in a field of curly, black grass. I moved in for a closer look. "Oh my God. Where's the rest of it?"

"That's all there is, that's all there ever was. The most common term for it is micropenis," he said.

I tried to speak but at first all I could muster were a few incomprehensible sounds. For the first time in my life I was at a loss for words. I couldn't help but stare at it. "What? How?" I finally squeaked out.

"I had a prenatal hormone deficiency. If my parents hadn't been high through most of my childhood, it was the sixties after all, they might have noticed. There were small windows of opportunity for treatment at different ages. Unfortunately my parents missed them all. And now even as an adult, the doctors tell me that surgery would only be marginally successful."

"So it doesn't get any bigger? I mean, does it get hard or anything?"

"It gets hard; I get another inch out of it when it does. It's fully functional, it's just small."

My initial reaction had been shock. I had no idea what I would see when he dropped trow but once I knew that I wasn't dealing with anything freaky like a transgender or some sort of mutilation, I relaxed I was happy to see I was dealing with a regular old penis, albeit a tiny one, and now I couldn't resist the urge to touch it. I reached in to take hold of it but Randy recoiled and pulled his pants back up. "Whoa, what do you think you're doing?"

"Easy," I said. "I just wanted to touch it."

"Ever think of asking before you go grabbing?"

"First of all it was out there for the grabbing and second, when it comes to cock, no, I never ask, now bring it here."

"No, you've seen enough, it's not some novelty act."

"And I'm not going to treat it as one."

He was reluctant to move closer to me.

"Having a small pecker doesn't explain why you've had so little sex," I said.

"Of course it does. No one wants to sleep with a guy who needs a magnifying glass to take a piss. You women say size doesn't matter, but you're just lying, it matters a lot."

"So you've stayed away from women all these years because you think that's true? You're embarrassed?"

"I don't have to tell you what it's like, you've been around rock stars for a long time. You've got people like Tommy Lee and Vince Neil showing off in videos; there are certain expectations."

"That's all in your head. Do you know how many rock star dicks I've seen?"

"Thousands?"

"That was a rhetorical question; it didn't require an answer."

"Sorry."

"Let me tell you from experience, there are a lot more small cocks out there than you think. Most of those guys, all they care about is sticking it into as many hot, wet, and cozy places as they can every night. And you'd probably be surprised at how many women want to let them do it no matter what."

"And you're one of them?"

"And I'm one of them," I said as I unzipped his pants. I slid them down past his massive thighs and got down on my knees. I swirled my tongue around the head of the little guy and wrapped my thumb and forefinger around the stump of what should have been a tree trunk. He was right – God is cruel.

It was rock hard and I could tell I was going to get the full two inches. I took it all in my mouth. I was halfway expecting he would have the response time of a 14-year-old boy and sure as shit, within seconds, he blew a load down my throat with no warning. And it was a full load in no way proportionate to the size of the unit from which it spewed.

I looked up at him and saw fear on his face. "I... I'm sorry he muttered."

I'm sure he was worried that he had violated some sort of blow job protocol. Maybe, but under the circumstances I didn't see the harm. I had been expecting it, after all. I wanted to make him feel at ease. I stood and smiled, "It's okay," I whispered. I kissed him gently on the lips and led him toward the bed. He lay down on his back and I liberated him from the rest of his clothes. Except for the obvious, the rest of his body was absolutely magnificent. It was not going to matter if he had two inches or twelve – I just wanted him inside me.

We fucked all afternoon and into the evening and even after blowing his wad with my initial blow job, he was still able to come three more times over the next eight hours. I'll be honest, it wasn't the best sex I'd ever had but it certainly wasn't the worst. On our third go-round, after faking two orgasms, I actually had a real one. That was quite a pleasant surprise.

Around 11 he got out of bed to go piss. At this point I felt he had given all he had to give so I decided to get dressed and call it a night. He came out of the bathroom just as I was finishing up.

"What's this? Where are you going," he asked.

"It's been a nice time," I said, "but I need to go."

"No you don't; stay the night with me."

"I can't, Randy."

"Why not?" he walked up and lovingly put his hands around my waist.

"Randy, no."

"What? I've never felt this way before. You've given me confidence and a whole new perspective on my life. I really think we could have something special."

Shit, I was afraid that would happen. If I had a nickel for every rock star that thought they had fallen for me during sex, I'd have just enough for a roll about the size of Randy's pecker.

"Look dude, I had a great time, I really did, and I'm glad you think I've helped you, but I'm not relationship girl. I'm one-night-stand-rock-star-fucker-girl. That's all I've ever been and all I aspire to be."

"It doesn't have to be like that."

"Yes it does," I said. I stood on tip-toes and gave him a long sensuous kiss on the lips then headed for the door.

"Wait. What about the interview? What are you going to write?"

"How about I just review the show? That's what they pay me for anyway," I said.

"So you'll be there tomorrow night?"

"Yes," I said.

"Okay, maybe I'll see you then."

"Sure," I said, knowing full well I wouldn't.

I left Randy's suite a satisfied woman. Not because the sex was satisfying but because the conquest was. Sure, there were a few scary moments as well as some unusual surprises but that's how most of these encounters are. I guess I kind of like it that way.

The next night I went to the Beavertrap show. The band was fantastic and Randy's vocals were phenomenal. I think the guys were even better now than they were in their '80's heyday. I wrote them a killer review.

HIGH SCHOOL (REUNION, NOT A MUSICAL)

"Do you think Wendy will be there?" There it was – the question either Bill or I was going to ask sooner or later. I just wished it hadn't been me. And I doubly wished it hadn't come in the first hour of a seven-hour road trip to our twenty-year high school reunion.

"She wasn't at any of the other ones, it's hard to say," Bill replied.

The girl in question was someone we had both been in love with in high school – at least I'm pretty sure he had been; we've never talked about it. I don't have any idea how far he went with her sexually or even if he knows how far I went. I wondered how often, if at all, he's thought about it over the years. All I know for sure is that neither of us has had contact with her in eighteen years.

Bill and I have been friends since pre-school, some thirty-four years, a long time for people our age. We didn't really hang together much during our junior high and high school years. We had different friends and hung around with very different groups but we always shared a bond of time and history.

The friendship almost crashed and burned twice. The first time was when we worked in a deli together in high school. I caught him hiding in the cooler drinking pilfered beers on the job. I was worried that we would both get the boot, so I turned him in. He got fired and we didn't talk for about a year. Then later on when he became a born-again Christian and wouldn't quit proselytizing at every opportunity, I put my foot down. I didn't want to hear it. We didn't talk for about six months that time. We got past all that stuff, though, and haven't had a single disagreement in sixteen years.

We grew up in Savannah, Georgia but somehow both ended up in south Florida. He became a minister for a Pentecostal church in Fort Lauderdale and I went to work for a Spanish language radio group in Miami. I spend my free time partying in South Beach; he spends his with his wife and three kids helping drug addicts find Jesus. Our lives could not be more different yet we somehow we've remained friends.

We had met Wendy in seventh grade. She was adorable with her brown hair, blue eyes and freckles that would all bunch together when she smiled. I fell hard and quick. She took to me right away as well and we became inseparable, though, for some reason, we never considered ourselves boyfriend and girlfriend.

Wendy and I stayed close all the way through tenth grade but at some point during the summer before eleventh grade, we started to fight a lot and grew apart pretty fast. We both had gotten drivers licenses and cars and, I guess, a taste of freedom. About this time she had also joined the high school band, which was a pretty tight-knit group. I wasn't welcome and frankly, I didn't care because I had no love for the band freaks. We had come close to sleeping together twice but I got as far as feeling her up through her shirt only to have her chicken out both times. I wanted it bad, but I never could find a way to close the deal. My first love had drifted away.

One day early on in our senior year, I saw Wendy's car parked in front of Bill's house after school. I found this strange. I knew they knew each other, it was a small town, everybody knew each other, but I didn't think it was well enough for her to be over at his place. He wasn't in the band and they had very little in common as far as I could tell. It didn't make any sense. From that day on, she was there almost every single school day until graduation. In fact, they even walked together at graduation. The school let the graduates choose whom they walked with so it became like a prom or a date situation that was taken very seriously. I never asked either of them about the nature of their relationship - probably because I didn't want to know the answer, but it's something that's bugged me for twenty years.

Wendy and I eventually got back to where we could relate on a friendly level again but were never as close at we once were. She eventually got married to someone neither Bill nor I knew and moved to Missouri. Bill was invited to her wedding; I was not.

"Man, I haven't thought about Wendy in years," Bill said.

"No?" I asked, not quite believing him.

"No, not really." He leaned forward and folded his arms across the steering wheel. He smiled a slight smile. "Man, did I have a crush on her."

"Oh yeah? I didn't know that," I lied. I tried to act nonchalant.

"She was such a blessing in my life."

Yeah, I'll bet, I thought. I really regretted bringing up the subject so I abruptly changed it and started playing a game we had played on many a road trip over the years. "What do you call a man with no arms and no legs hanging on the wall?"

"Art," he said. "Here's one I just thought of. What do you call a man with no arms or legs breaking into your car?"

"Unsuccessful?"

"Jimmy," he said laughing.

"Good one," I said. It was going to be a long ride up to Savannah.

****

We had decided we were going to make this trip as cheap as possible. Neither of us really wanted to shell out $100 a person to attend the reunion. He didn't drink and I was a vegetarian so neither of us was going to get our money's worth food and drink-wise. Neither of us had family or close friends in Savannah anymore so we were going to need to stay in a motel. The whole thing was going to cost a small fortune so we thought we'd save some money by driving, splitting the gas and sharing a motel room.

It was two in the afternoon when we pulled into the Comfort Inn on the outskirts of town. We decided showers were in order to cleanse ourselves of the road dirt, then maybe a cruise of the old haunts around town and an early dinner on our own.

We got cleaned up and headed for our old elementary school. We were walking through the playground area near the rear of the classrooms when Bill decided to revisit the Wendy topic. "Why did you bring up Wendy before?"

Shit, I really didn't want to talk about this anymore. "I don't know," I lied. "Just making conversation."

"Uh huh," he said, not really buying it.

We walked past our old 5th grade classroom. "Remember when Larry Brooks threw Justin McBride through this window?" I asked.

"Like it was yesterday. You had it pretty bad for her didn't you?"

I took a second to figure out how I wanted to answer the question. Did I want to lie or not? Fuck it. We've known each other a long time; I might as well come clean. "Yeah... like you don't even know."

"I knew. Everybody did."

I laughed. "Yeah, I guess they did."

We walked past the monkey bars. "Isn't this where you fell off the bars and lost your front tooth?" he said.

"No, that was across the street at the park. I broke my arm on this one."

"You sure?"

"Painfully sure."

We walked a few more steps in silence, barely remembering what it was like to be a kid again. "You ever do her?" he asked out of left field.

Whoa! To say I was shocked would be an understatement. Did he just drop the same question that's been on my mind for twenty years? I didn't know how to respond, I just looked at him with my jaw on the ground.

"What? You've never heard a minister say 'do'?"

"Funny."

"So did you?"

"No... You?

He didn't respond right away, which made me really nervous. Then finally while looking straight ahead he answered. "No." Then he kind of laughed and looked at me curiously. "Why would you think that?"

"Why was her car parked at your house every day?"

"You thought we had a thing?"

"Didn't you?"

Bill burst out laughing. "Man, I was either drunk or high so much in those days I couldn't get it up if I tried. Don't you remember who I lived next door to?"

"No."

"You don't remember that band loser, Jason German?"

We had made it back to the car. I stood at the door waiting for him to finish. "She was fucking his brains out," he said all casual. He smirked and entered the car. Once again I was stunned. Did I just hear a Pentecostal minister say "fuck"?

The automatic window rolled down in front of me. "What's the matter? You've never heard a minister say 'brains' before?"

****

After cruising past both of our childhood homes and making similar complaints about how crappy they looked now compared to the way our parents had kept them up, we went to dinner. We settled on a Greek place that we used to go to. The name was the same but the owners were different. Thankfully the food was just as good as we remembered.

Bill seemed determined to keep the Wendy topic alive for as long as possible. "What would you have said if I had told you I was having sex with her?"

"I'm not sure. It's disturbing enough to know that Jason German was sleeping with her. It gives me the willies just thinking about it. I still remember what he looked like with that gross straight, stiff, hair-sprayed hair and those gay turtlenecks he wore.

Bill laughed. He remembered exactly what I was talking about. "And that car he drove. Remember the 'yoke'… that bright yellow Chevette?"

"The 'vet that got 'em wet."

"It got *her* wet apparently."

"Apparently," I said with disgust. "I don't get it. What did she see in that guy?"

"Who knows? The fact is, she was a very unhappy girl in general. She hated Savannah, she had a crappy home life and couldn't wait to leave. Maybe she saw him as a ticket out of here. He had a full ride music scholarship to USC that he wound up losing because of his coke habit."

"Oops." I chuckled. "What a shame."

We each ordered a baklava and wolfed them down pretty quick. While we were waiting for the check, I asked him how he happened to know so much about everything.

"She did come over occasionally when she wanted some pot or something. We were pretty good friends, she used to spill her guts. I didn't really care, I just wanted someone, anyone, to get messed up with."

"She ever mention me?"

The check arrived and we both tried to take possession. "I'll get this one," he said. "You get breakfast."

That was fine with me. Breakfast would be cheaper anyway.

I had forgotten about my last question to him until we were parking outside the ballroom of the Sheraton where the reunion was being held. "You never said whether Wendy mentioned me or not."

"Maybe we should save this for the trip back."

"Why? Was it bad?"

Just then a heavyset woman walked by with a skinny bald guy. Bill did a double take. "Whoa, did you see who that was?"

"Kind of looked like Michelle what's-her-name, the head cheerleader."

"Exactly," Bill said. "She's not looking to hot, looks like she put on about a hundred bucks."

"Maybe a hundred and a half," I said.

"And who was the dude?"

"I think he was the kicker from the football team. What self-respecting head cheerleader winds up with the kicker?"

He laughed and opened the door to get out.

"Wait a minute," I said. "What did she say about me?"

"It was along time ago. It doesn't really matter anymore does it?"

"It does to me."

He closed the door and looked at me seriously. "She said you had jealousy issues."

"What?" I said, shocked. "That is so not true!"

"C'mon, man, you used to get so pissed whenever she talked to any guy that wasn't you."

"No I didn't."

He shrugged his shoulders. "Whatever. You wanted to know. I'm just telling you what she said."

"Yeah, well you were drunk and high. You probably misunderstood what she was saying."

"I don't think so."

I opened the door and got out. "Well, if she's here, I'm saying something."

"That's your call. She probably won't be, though."

I was kind of annoyed now. It was not a good way to start off a party. He was right though, she wasn't likely to show up so I tried to put it out of my mind and get into party mode.

****

Over the next several hours, I exchanged pleasantries with about 200 people, answered the same where have you been, what are you doing now questions over and over, met about a hundred spouses and had a few more drinks than I should have. Overall I was having a good time. Wendy never made it to the reunion. It was the only thing I was disappointed about.

Bill and I had stuck together for a while but he ran into some of the people he used to get high with and went to find out if they had found Jesus yet.

A couple of hours in, he sauntered up and asked me how it was going and if I was planning on staying for a while.

"I'm having a good time," I said. "I'll probably stay a couple hours. Why?"

"I've got kind of a headache, I'm thinking of turning in early."

"Okay. Will it bother you if I come in late?"

"Nah, I'm a heavy sleeper. How will you get back?"

"I'll get a ride, don't worry about it. Feel better, I'll see you later."

Not ten minutes after he left, I started feeling queasy. Maybe it was the hummus from dinner mixed with Southern Comfort I'd been tossing back, I don't know but it was coming on quick. I excused myself to the restroom and barely made it to a stall before I blew chunks.

That didn't make me feel one bit better so I decided I'd better get back to the room so I could hopefully sleep off whatever it was before we left for home. I got Justin McBride, the guy who'd been thrown through the classroom window as a kid, to give me a ride. We had to pull over once during the ten-minute drive so I could puke on the side of the road. I was really hoping it was just an alcohol thing rather than food poisoning.

When we got to the motel I thanked Justin for the ride and promised to stay in touch like I do at every reunion then don't. As I neared the top of the stairs, I felt it coming on again. I needed to make a quick decision to either try for the room or find an out-of-the-way place outside. I went for the room. I slipped my key card into the slot and shoved the door open. Normally, I would have tried to be really quiet but it just wasn't possible considering the state I was in.

I burst into the room, sprinted toward the bathroom but then stopped dead in my tracks when I saw what was going on. Bill was right in the middle of fucking the shit out of some woman. I couldn't hold it in. I sprayed vomit all over the floor and part of the dresser. Bill and the woman stopped what they were doing to look at me in shock. When I saw that the woman was Wendy, I puked again, this time all over his bed.

She screamed out some cuss words that I don't remember now, leapt out of bed and scrambled for her clothes. I caught a glimpse of her while she hurriedly dressed. She looked as good naked now as I'd imagined she did twenty years ago.

"Holy fucking shit!" I screamed. I lost my balance and grabbed onto the TV to keep from falling.

Bill pulled his pants on and came to my aid. "Let's get you into the bathroom. I'll get some towels."

He led me into the bathroom where I knelt down in front of the toilet. He grabbed all of the towels and went to clean up the mess. I heard the front door open and then some whispering that I couldn't quite make out. It seemed to be Wendy doing most of the talking.

My heart was racing, my head was spinning and my stomach was turning. It was too much. I must have passed out at that point because the next thing I remember was the cold water from the shower hitting my face. I was sitting up in the tub, fully clothed with Bill knocking chunks of barf off my clothes with a washcloth. My stomach was feeling better but then I suddenly remembered the scene I had walked in on and started to get really pissed. "Is she still here?"

"No," he said.

"You're fucking unbelievable!" I screamed. "You're a Goddamn liar and a hypocrite."

The shower was really getting on my nerves. I scrambled to get out of there. It was awkward and slippery. I slipped and slid a few times before getting it right. Bill backed way off, not knowing if I would take a swing at him or what I would do. "Unbelievable. That wasn't the first time was it?"

He looked down at the ground, ashamed.

"Was it?" I screamed louder.

"No."

"See, this is what I don't get about you hardcore religious freaks. You think you can do whatever you want and as long as you ask God for forgiveness you think you've got a guaranteed spot in heaven or whatever. You are quite the role model for your congregation aren't you?"

I was starting to feel extremely uncomfortable in my wet clothes so I stripped down and put on a t-shirt and a pair of shorts.

"You don't know the whole story," he said.

"I don't care what your fucking story is. In fact, I can't even be around you right now." I started to gather up my things.

"What are you doing?"

"I'm packing my shit and I'm going to get another room."

"No, stay. I'll go get another room. You shouldn't have to move, you're not feeling well."

I didn't disagree with him. He quickly packed his stuff and left. We agreed to meet at the car at eight the next morning. I didn't know how I was going to handle being in the car with him all the way back to south Florida.

****

The next morning, thankfully, I felt a lot better. I assumed my illness was caused by a bad mixture of food and alcohol. Bill and I met at the car promptly at eight. We decided against going somewhere for breakfast. At this point we both just wanted to get the hell out of Savannah. After the breakfast decision we didn't speak to each other at all until we crossed into Florida almost two hours later.

"You're probably not interested in anything I have to say right now..." he began.

"You're right about that," I said.

"I feel I owe you an explanation."

"You think?"

There was a long pause before he spoke again. I watched and waited. He tried to speak several times but seemed to be having trouble finding the right words.

Finally he found some. "You're right that I've been a hypocrite. I've taken advantage of my relationship with God time and time again. I've committed sin after sin and have always blamed God for giving me free will but no willpower. I always believed that He would either help me or forgive me. I've had to rely on forgiveness because I've been a weak, helpless addict my entire life. Thankfully He sent help for my drug and alcohol addiction in the form of my wife, Stephanie. She came along at a time where if I'd kept going the way I was, I would have been dead six months out of high school. She had a relationship with Jesus that was unbreakable. She helped me find Him and for the last eighteen years we have devoted our lives to Jesus and the church."

"Okay, so what's the problem?"

"The problem was that while I thought I had kicked my addictions, I really only transferred them from one thing to another. I became addicted to sex."

"So? You had Stephanie."

"Yes but what you don't know is that we never slept together until our wedding night. That was a full two years after we'd met."

"But you guys lived together and even slept in the same bed all that time."

"Yeah and she wouldn't give it up because it was a sin in the eyes of God."

"No shit," I said. "But how does Wendy fit in."

"Well, one of the things I needed to do to get off drugs was to get rid of the people in my life who were a part of the problem. She was one of them but she would not let go so easy. She was a major pot head and I was her main connection. She knew about Stephanie's ban on sex and that I was horny as hell, so she thought she could screw me back into dealing. Eventually, I was able to help her get clean, she met a nice guy and moved away. But just so you know, we never slept together until after I got clean. Most of those times you saw her car in front of my house, she was actually at Jason German's house."

"Okay, so you guys just ran into each other here and decided to take up where you left off?"

"Not exactly, we never actually ended it."

"What do you mean you never ended it?"

"I mean we fell in love and have been together ever since."

I couldn't believe what I was hearing. "How? How have you been together all this time?"

"Coincidentally, my church's national organization is based in Missouri - about a half hour from where she lives in St. Louis. I fly up there for meetings for a few days every quarter and we meet up then."

"Jesus."

"Yeah."

"So what now?" I asked. "Did you guys break it off or what?"

"Why would we do that? Because you caught us?"

"Uh, yeah."

"I told you, we've been together for almost two decades. You can't just end it, there's history there, just like with you and me."

"And your wife."

"Yes, and I would never leave her either. I love them both. I love you all. It's a curse I've had to live with."

"Yeah, I feel real bad for you. Can you see the tears running down my face?"

Bill shook his head and watched the road unfold in front of us. "Maybe Mormonism would have been a better fit for you," I said. That was the last thing that was said for quite a while.

As the morning wore on and the distance between us and Savannah increased I began to lighten up and even feel a little sorry for Bill. This was a guy with some serious issues - issues that I was happy as hell to not have. I wondered what would have happened if Wendy and I would have ended up together. I'm not sure I would have had what it took to help her get clean, much less stay that way. I guess I should be happy that they both had someone to help save their lives. Who am I to judge what they've been doing? I live a life full of sin myself, too many women, too many parties, too much swearing, I've even been "the other man" a time or two.

Bill has helped a lot of people in a lot of ways over the years and even though he's a minister, he's a human first and foremost. It's stupid to let my jealousy, and that's what it boils down to be - jealousy - ruin a friendship that has endured for more than thirty years. I should just shut the fuck up, be there to listen if he needs it, help him if I can and thank God that I finally got to see Wendy naked.

At that moment I did not have the courage to voice my newly adopted view so I just continued to sit quietly. Man-love is not an easy thing to put out there.

As we passed the last Daytona exit, Bill spoke again. "Look," he said. "I'm not sure what I can say to make you understand. All I can do is finally be honest..."

"Just stop okay? All I want is the answer to one question."

"What's that?" he said.

"What do you call a man with no arms and no legs under a car?"

"I don't know, what?"

"Jack."

"Good one," he said. We both laughed. It would be a long ride back to south Florida.

THE DAY I CREATED THE NAKED MONSTER

"No! I won't do it," Jill yelled. "I'm not going to prance around like some stripper."

Jill was such a baby. It was just the two of us for God's sake. It's not like it was a bar full of people. It was our bedroom where we made love nearly every night for the past two years except for sick days and menstrual periods. "Oh, come on, it'll be fun," I said.

"Yeah? Fun for who?"

"For both of us. It'll be like this whole role-playing thing. You'll be the hot stripper and I'll be the hot customer that you can't keep your hands off of even though it's against the rules."

"How about I play the Arabian princess who has to keep her body covered or else she gets beheaded and you can be the U.S. Marine who's come to take me away to America?"

"Okay, but as soon as I bust you out, I'm just going to want to rip your clothes off and make mad passionate love on the sands of the

Mojave. Either way, I'm getting you naked," I said as I pulled her in close and tried to unbutton her blouse.

"Okay, first of all I think you mean the Sahara because the Mojave's in California. Second of all, the Sahara's in Africa, not Saudi Arabia. I seriously thought you Marines knew your geography better than that."

"Well, I'm not really a Marine."

"And I'm not really going to run around naked," she said as she pulled away and headed for the bathroom.

I sank down on the bed, dejected as usual. "I don't get it, baby, you're gorgeous, you have a phenomenal, sexy body. Why are you so ashamed of it?"

"I'm not ashamed of it, Bobby," she said as she emerged from the bathroom dressed in her usual un-sexy flannel nightgown. "I'm just not comfortable with nakedness. I can't explain it, it's just the way I feel."

She crawled into bed and pulled the covers up under her chin. I just shook my head in disbelief. I stripped naked and was about to get into bed. "Umm, what did I just say?" she asked. "It's not just my nakedness, it's everyone's."

"Sorry. Geez." I put my skivvies back on and climbed into bed.

She turned off the light and we lay on our backs and stared at the ceiling for a moment. "Well, what are you waiting for? I'm ready," she said.

I was no longer in the mood. For two years we'd been doing it in the dark, under the covers with that stupid nightgown pulled up to her neck. In the time we've been together I've only seen her naked three times, and two of those were accidents. I wanted to add some spice to our sex life. I wanted to come home early from work and sneak up on her while she was making dinner then do that thing they do in the movies where they sweep everything from the table and have wild, sweaty sex right there in the kitchen. I wanted to do it standing up in the shower, or on the couch in the living room, or in the car in the garage. I wanted some variety. I was getting bored.

"Sorry, baby, I just remembered I've got an early meeting," I said.

"Oh. Okay. G'night then," she said. She kissed me on the cheek then snuggled up next to me. Spooning would be all that would happen tonight. Something had to change.

****

"Bobby, you should have been there. It was amazing," Roger said, as he danced into my office. He probably shouldn't be dancing at his age. He wasn't really in the greatest shape.

"I've been to Miami Beach before," I said. "In fact, I have to go down next week to work on the Telemundo account. What's the big deal?"

"The big deal is I went to a different place this time. A place called Haulover Beach."

"So?"

"So, it's a nude beach. It's not just topless, it's all nude, all the time!" Roger was bursting with excitement. "You ever been to a nude beach before?"

"Can't say as I have."

"Well, my friend, you have no idea what you're missing."

"Yeah? So you go native or what?"

"That's the best part, you don't have to. You can keep your clothes on and nobody cares."

"That's kind of chickenshit, don't you think?"

"Aw, come on, man, gimme a break," he said. "Can't you ever just let an old guy have his float in the parade without raining all over it?"

I chuckled to myself. He was right. "Sorry. So where is this place? How did you find it?"

"It's a couple miles north of South Beach. I was just walking along and all of a sudden, BAM, everyone was naked. My God, the women..."

"I'll make sure I check it out when I'm there. Haulover, you say?"

"Yeah," he said. "Amazing place, amazing place."

He left my office with his head in the clouds. He even resumed his little dance as he headed down the hallway. The sad thing was I could see myself getting overly excited about stuff like that when I get to be his age, especially if my bland sex life continued the way it was.

****

I sometimes took Jill on business trips with me, especially if it was to someplace fun and interesting or in this case, warm. It had been a long winter in Chicago and we both needed a break from the frigid conditions.

These trips were usually more like paid vacations. I'd go somewhere for two or three days, do the usual meet and greets, put in some face time and basically the rest of the time was mine. When Jill was with me we'd usually use that time to eat or sightsee or shop. And boy could that girl shop. She used our spare bedroom as one big closet for all her clothes. When we were in Miami though, it was all about the beach and in keeping with her modest ways she always wore a one-piece swimsuit and a sarong.

The morning of our second day there, I woke her before the sun came up. "Come on, baby, get your stuff, we're going to the beach," I said.

"But it's still dark out," she whined groggily.

"I know. I've got a surprise."

****

We stood in the middle of the deserted beach just as the sun was peeking up from the horizon. "It's beautiful," she said.

"Thank you," I replied.

"For what? You didn't do anything?" She looked at me and suddenly knew what I was talking about. She saw that I had taken off my swim trunks and was standing there buck naked.

"Oh my God! What are you doing?" She freaked out. "Put your shorts back on for God's sake! You are going to get in so much trouble!"

"It's okay. You can do that here. It's a nude beach," I said.

"It's a what?"

"A nude beach. Come on, there's no one around, give it a shot."

"I can't believe you brought me to a nude beach! What the hell were you thinking?" She turned and stormed off toward the parking lot.

"I was thinking I wanted to save this marriage," I yelled after her.

She stopped, turned around and looked at me like I had just called her a whore or something. "Save it? Save it from what? Is it in danger?" she asked.

"Yes, it is. I can't go on like this."

"Like what? I thought everything was fine."

I walked toward her. "Well it's not," I said.

She looked away. "Could you put your shorts on please? I can't talk to you when you're all... hanging around like that."

"See, that's the problem right there," I said. "I want us to be more adventurous when it comes to things like this... things like our sex life. I used to think all this modesty was cute, but you know what? It's not cute anymore. It's downright annoying."

The beach was starting to fill up with people pretty quick. People of all shapes and sizes were picking out their patch of sand and shedding their clothes all around us.

"I want us to be free," I said. "Free to explore new things, to not care who might be watching. I want us to shed our inhibitions and add some excitement to our lives. I'm bored, baby, and if things don't change..."

"If things don't change what? What are you going to do?

"I don't know exactly. I'd just hate to have to find excitement elsewhere."

She was getting pissed. She turned red with anger.

"See, look at that guy," I said, pointing to a huge fat guy who had to weigh about three hundred bucks. "If there's anybody who should be ashamed to be naked it's him." Then he turned around and revealed the biggest schlong I'd ever seen. "On second thought, don't look at him. He's a bad example."

"So what are you saying? You'll leave me? Cheat on me? What?" She said, clearly upset.

"Well... I..." I instantly regretted my decision to handle things this way. I had no answer.

"Okay, you want naked, I'll give you naked." She dropped her beach chair and tote bag and peeled off her sweatshirt. "You want the whole world to see me? You want all these creepy old men to ogle me? You got it pal!" Off came the shorts.

When she put it that way I suddenly didn't like where the discussion was headed. I was going to get my way but now I wasn't sure I wanted it. "Listen, maybe I was a little hasty..."

"Maybe? You think?" She wiggled out of her swimsuit and threw it in my face. "Satisfied?" she asked, standing there more naked than I've ever seen.

She wasn't really calming down like I'd hoped and frankly, I'd never seen her that mad. It was like something inside her snapped. She did look good, though. This was the first time in two years of marriage and one year of courtship that I'd seen her fully naked in broad daylight. She was amazing. I couldn't believe what I'd been missing all these years.

"Let's show everyone, shall we?" she said. "I'm going for a run."

"Okay, Baby, you made your point. I was wrong, I'm sorry. Here, you can put this back on now." I held out her suit, hoping she'd take it.

"Not on your life," she said and jogged away toward the majority of beachgoers.

"She'll calm down," I said out loud to no one. I put my swim trunks back on. Suddenly I was the one embarrassed to be naked. I set up the beach chairs and positioned myself so I could watch what she was doing. What she seemed to be doing was making new friends.

She stopped and talked to every person she jogged by, shook hands then moved on to the next.

I sat by myself for an hour. I couldn't concentrate on my book, I couldn't enjoy the view and I couldn't help but think about how I could have done this better. Anyone who thought the Mojave was in Saudi Arabia probably should have thought the whole plan through a little better.

When Jill finally showed up I couldn't tell right away what kind of mood she was in. I had laid out her swimsuit across the beach chair hoping she'd put it on right away.

"Hey," she said with a smile. She ignored the suit and sat down on top of it.

"Hey," I said, unsure how to proceed. "Towel?"

"No thanks."

"So, umm... you about ready to go?"

"No. Could you hand me my book please?"

I handed her the whole bag. "So, uhh... you still mad?"

She opened her book. "Nope. Not at all."

"You sure?"

She looked up and straight ahead like I was bothering her and she was tired of it. She snapped the book shut.

"Look," she said. "Just like you, I hate to admit when I'm wrong. But this time you were right and I should thank you."

"For?" I was perplexed and intrigued.

"For liberating me."

Whoa! I hadn't seen that coming.

"I have never felt so free," she said. "I don't know why I was so hung up on my body. Or anyone else's for that matter. I feel like a whole new me. Thanks, Baby." She leaned over, kissed me on the cheek and that was it. She went back to her book while I sat there stunned.

****

I wish I could say that the story ended right there and everything turned out fairy-tale perfect, but I can't. In fact, it was just the beginning of a downhill slide that I still can't see the end of. I not only created a monster, but a naked one of all things.

That day on the beach, Jill became obsessed with nakedness. Now she does almost everything naked. She cooks and cleans naked; watches TV naked and she even answers the door naked. She shed her clothes for Mother's Day at my mom's house. She stripped for Father's Day at her dad's house. She exposed herself to little Ira Cohen at his bar mitzvah.

She started to sunbathe naked in the backyard every afternoon during the summer. When the traffic reporters for the local TV stations found out, they started to fly their helicopters over our yard to take pictures. One day there was a serious near miss, which prompted the FAA to give her a warning. Then the FCC tried to fine her after some of the sunbathing footage accidentally ended up on the air. She's been arrested fourteen times for indecent exposure and has been on Howard Stern twice.

I'm not quite sure what I should do besides ride it out. After all, I started this whole thing. I'm the one who wanted adventure. Well, I'm getting it now, man. The only upside to all this is at least she doesn't spend all our money on clothes anymore.

THE AIRPORT READING MATERIAL INCIDENT

Unwritten rules are complete bullshit. I've come to the conclusion that, somewhere, somehow there is some sort of a "Book of Life" or something that I have not read. And apparently I'm the only one because it seems that I cannot do a single thing right in the eyes of society. I thought the only real rules we needed to pay attention to were on those stone tablets that came down the mountain with Charlton Heston. I only remember a couple of them but at least they are the big ones. You know, the ones about killing and stealing and something about not coveting thy neighbors wife, though truth be told, she coveted me first and it was only a couple of times. But let me tell you, unwritten my ass - they're written down somewhere, and believe me, they're fucked up.

Looking back, I think my father may have been an expert on the life book, or at least thought he was. The same guy who used to insist I wear a suit and tie on an airplane and refused to take me out in public if I was wearing shorts as a kid, owned the most hideous collection of plaid slacks known to man. He looked like President Ford on a golf outing – every fucking day. I don't care if it was the 70's, it didn't make it right. Anyway, he seemed to have the answer for everything and tried to hold me to an impossible standard. I mean who really gives a shit whether an 8-year-old wears shorts to McDonalds or not? I would question it and he'd either say "because I said so" or "It's an unwritten rule and you need to learn it."

I think it was a childhood filled with ridiculous shit like that that causes me to wear shorts and busy Hawaiian shirts to weddings and funerals today. If my father hadn't been cremated he'd surely be flopping around in his grave. Then again, he might very well be yelling I told you so from the great beyond right now. Why would he be doing that? Because I'm sitting here in airport jail thanks to another one of those unwritten rules I was unaware of.

It had been another glorious weekend in Las Vegas with what I call "the 3 g's" – golf, gambling, and girls, also known as frustration, losing and strippers. Anyway, I was sitting in the airport, minding my own business when it was announced that my short flight back to L.A. would be delayed because of snow in Albuquerque. I always caught the last flight out of Vegas so I could squeeze out every possible minute of debauchery. My two friends had done the smart thing and caught the afternoon flight back. But no, not me, my strategy was now going bite me in the ass. I would have to sit and wait, exhausted and broke, for at least another two hours.

Being the Vegas airport, there was no end of things to do to pass the time. There were plenty of slot machines and places to get a drink but frankly, I had gone a little overboard on this trip and was thoroughly sick of both. I decided to peruse the gift shop for some reading material.

I didn't want a novel, it would take me three years to read it and most of them had Fabio or somebody like him on the cover anyway (not my thing.) I didn't want a newspaper, it would just get my hands dirty and I could scan all that bullshit in about five minutes anyway. It would have to be a magazine, but which one, that was the question.

The shelves were filled with all kinds of crap I would never read: *Newsweek, Cosmo, Popular Mechanics, People* - the usual stuff. I was about to give up and go for a novel after all when the black plastic-wrapped magazine on the top shelf in the back caught my eye. I picked it up and took a closer look. Ah, *Playboy*, now we were talking, I hadn't read one of those in years. I'd gotten my fill of two of the three "g's" this weekend - the golf and the gambling - but the girls, how could one possibly get sick of them? I paid the ancient woman at the counter (who shot me a disgusted look, by the way) and headed off the nether regions of Terminal C's Gate 21.

I tore into the plastic and freed the magazine. Paris Hilton was on the cover. Jesus Christ. I hoped to God that she wasn't naked in there, I'd seen enough of her bony ass and bare twat in her sex video. A quick flip through the pages revealed that thankfully, she was not.

There were, however, plenty of blonde Paris Hilton look-alikes. That was one of the problems with Playboy these days - it was almost exclusively blondes. Don't get me wrong, if the only snatch around is a blonde one I'll take it, but in my opinion, brunettes are just plain hot. I miss the old days of *Playboy* when Barbi Benton and Candy Loving, both gorgeous brunettes, seemed to be in every issue.

The other thing I miss is actually seeing some pussy. As I flipped through, I could see they didn't show as much as they used to - it was mostly just big, fake tits and ass. Again, I remember back in the good old days when all these Playmates had full, wild bushes - the kind you just wanted to bury your face in and stay there all day. Now not only are they all shaved, but you can barely see any gash at all.

I turned to the *Playmate of the Month*. This one looked like Pam Anderson (she's another one I could do without). I skipped her biography since I figured it would just be the same old thing where she describes her turn-ons and turn-offs and all that. Who really gives a fuck anyway? I set the magazine in my lap and took a peek at the centerfold. The picture was totally lame and tame. It was one of those shots where she stood looking back over her shoulder with her bare ass to the camera. No nipples, no nothing. Needless to say, I was kind of disgusted.

It was about then that I heard a man loudly clear his throat. I could feel a presence in front of me. I looked up from the magazine and there stood a mild-mannered father-type in a subtle Hawaiian shirt, khaki shorts and Birkenstocks glaring down at me. I looked up at him. "Can I help you with something?" I asked.

"Can I ask you to put that filth away?"

I was stunned. Was he talking about the *Playboy*? "Filth? This?"

"Yeah, that. This is a public place and my wife and kids shouldn't have to be exposed to that kind of trash," he said as he pointed at his wife and what looked to be two boys about 10 and 12. I turned around and saw that the entire family was wearing the exact same Hawaiian print, the boys in shirts and the wife in a pretty sundress. She was clearly upset and hiding the eyes of the 10-year-old while the 12-year-old appeared to be very interested in trying to catch a glimpse of my magazine.

"This is Vegas, there's worse things on the cabs," I said.

"I can't do anything about that, but I can certainly ask you to not to read that in the airport."

My blood was starting to boil but I was surprising myself by staying calm. Normally I might have decked the asshole, but I was way too fucking tired and I wasn't quite sure if it was a federal offense to hit a guy in an airport. "Where am I supposed to read it?"

"I don't know, but this is clearly not the place."

"Well, you know, it's not really all that clear to me." I set the *Playboy* down cover up then stood and casually stuck my hands in my pockets. Totally non-threatening in my mind but I was tired of looking up at him, it had to be done.

He put his hands on his hips and looked away like he couldn't believe this wasn't going to be simple. Was he used to getting his way? Did he do stuff this stupid all of the time? He didn't know me. For all he knew I could just get up and whack him in his face. I glanced over at his wife. Brunette. Except for the hook-nose she was kind of cute. I think I'd rather see the staple through her navel than the Pammy look-alike with the big, fake titties.

"Look," he said. "What you do in private is your business, I totally respect that, but you cannot look at pornography in an airport."

"Why do they sell it at the airport then?"

"Who knows? I assume it's so you can take it back to your hotel and amuse yourself there."

"Oh really? You assume?" I looked over at the wife again. It was then that I noticed that she was sitting directly below a giant ad for the Rio Hotel - an ad that featured two scantily clad Brazilian showgirls showing far more than Pammy was in the centerfold. "That makes no sense," I said, turning back to him. "They sell this stuff at the airport so you can pass the time on your trip. You don't actually believe that someone is going to get off their plane in Vegas, head straight for the gift shop for a *Playboy* and then rush off to their hotel to go whack off do you?"

"You need to watch your language while you're at it."

I raised an eyebrow. "What language? What'd I say?"

Just then the wife came up and stood next to him. "You know what you said, I'm not going to repeat it," he said.

"Just forget it," the wife said to her husband, voice dripping with self-righteousness. "Let's just get security."

"Security?" These people were really starting to piss me off. "Are you fucking kidding me?"

"That's it, let's go," she said tugging his arm. "You had your chance," she said to me as she walked away yanking her husband along.

I was floored. Had that just happened? Did I really deserve this intrusion? Had I broken some law? I could vaguely make out the outline of a thong under her dress. Nice, I thought as I watched her loose cheeks sway back and forth, unencumbered from the support of full-assed panties. Great ass. Too bad it was attached to a cunt. I sat back down and picked up my reading material. I decided to check out the fiction section. If there was one thing Playboy still had going for it was a top-notch fiction section.

I barely got through the second paragraph of a story about a TV addict who passed up sex with the school slut to watch his favorite soap opera when I felt a presence again. I looked up and found two cops standing in front of me. They had guns on their hips and badges on their chests but they didn't really look like real cops, they were wearing shorts for Christ sake. Must be nice. Not much chance of getting shot on this job is there, Pal? "What's up, guys? What can I do for you tonight?" I already knew. More bullshit.

"Sir, we're going to have to ask you to put away your magazine," said the tall, skinny one with a nametag that said, Cabot.

"Can I ask why?"

"It's disturbing the passengers," the short, pudgy, angry one with Sergeant stripes said. His nametag read, Mostello.

I looked beyond him to see the husband and wife standing a few feet away with a pair of fuck you smiles. Speaking of pairs, I finally realized what great tits the wife had. She could almost be in Playboy. If it wasn't for that fucking hook-nose...

"Sir, it's disturbing the passengers," he repeated. I snapped back to the reality of my situation.

"It's not like I'm flashing it around, I'm just trying to sit and read peacefully. In fact, maybe I should file a complaint about them disturbing me.

"Disturbing you?" said Cabot.

"That's right. I think it's disturbing that they're all wearing the same clothes. I mean come on, there really oughtta be a law don't you think?" I said loud enough for the family to hear.

The tall, skinny one turned and looked at them, then looked back at me. I could tell he wanted to laugh; he knew I was right. The likely prospect that Sergeant Mostello would wring his neck kept him from doing it though.

"Very funny, Sir," Mostello said. "You're really trying my patience, now either put the magazine away or you're going to jail. It's that simple."

"All right, let me get this straight, it's illegal to read a men's magazine in public?"

Mostello put his hands on his knees and bent over to sneer in my face. "Have you ever seen anyone read one in public?"

I tried to think back. Come to think of it, no I hadn't. I found that a bit strange. Oh shit! This was another one of those fucking unwritten rules! I looked up at Cabot. He just shrugged his shoulders.

"No," I muttered.

"That's right and do you know why?"

"Unwritten rule?" I asked.

"That's right, unwritten rule... you just don't do it."

Damn it. Cabot and Mostello had me. I have stood up against unwritten rules many times before but this was the first time I was facing jail. Okay, it's airport jail, but still. At that moment I could have sworn I heard my old man cough out a dusty, smoky, ashy, I told you so.

"But the thing is, you're in trouble for disturbing the peace. That, my friend, is a very real rule," Mostello said. "So I'll ask you one more time, what's it going to be, stow the magazine or go to jail?"

Now here, is where most people would take the easy way out, chuck the magazine and be done with it.

"Okay, fine," I said. "You've left me with no choice." Mostello backed off. I stood up and again looked past them to the wife. Damn, she was hot. Even the fucking hook-nose was looking sexy now. I got a half-woody just thinking about how that nose would feel sliding across my balls. I took the *Playboy* and instead of shoving it in my bag, I held it up and let the centerfold fall open. I showed it to everyone at the gate because, of course, everyone at the gate was already watching the stupid asshole getting busted.

Cabot wasted no time grabbing the *Playboy* out of my hand and tossing it aside while Mostello wrestled me to the ground and cuffed me up. I was showing them, by God. Nobody was going to tell me what I could and couldn't read in the airport. Everyone at the gate started applauding. That's right, people, I'm doing it for you! I'm Norma fucking Rae!

Cabot and Mostello marched me past the family. I took one last look at the wife to make sure I had her image burned into my brain for later. I happened to glance over to where I had been sitting. While the husband and wife were waving a smug goodbye to me, their 12-year-old was slipping the discarded *Playboy* into his shirt. I laughed my ass off at that. The effects of my choice of reading material were going to be far-reaching in that family.

So here I am sitting in airport jail. Really it's just a regular, white, windowless room with a reinforced door. It's nothing really. Not much chance I'm going to get my cornhole violated in here (unless, of course, Cabot and Mostello decide to have their way with me). Cabot tells me I'll be out in a couple of hours, they'll issue me a citation and give me a date to see the judge in a month or so. That's cool, maybe I'll make a long weekend out of it and squeeze in the "3 g's". Damn, now I'm bored. If only I had some reading material.

TWO VERY DIFFERENT DANCES

Her Dance

It is a slow night at the club I dance at. It's the all-nude Booty's
"gentlemen's" club. If there was anyone else to approach for a lap
dance I would. If I didn't need to pay my rent tomorrow I would skip
it altogether and go home.

This isn't a big city strip club, it's Albuquerque and it's a
Tuesday. I don't usually work Tuesday nights but I had to this week
because of the whole not having money for rent thing. It doesn't
seem to matter that it's Two-for-Tuesday - two lap dances for the
price of one - the club is dead. The only people in the place are a
couple of rude, cheap-ass, Mexican gangbangers, a pair of dykes and
him. The bangers aren't going to spend any money and I don't lap
dance for girls. That just leaves him.

To an outsider, he probably seems like a nice, normal guy, well
groomed, in his early thirties but to someone who has made a living

as a "dancer" for more than three years as I have, I see something entirely different. I see a disgusting pervert loser.

I watch him from my procrastination stool at the bar. He probably thinks I'm checking him out. He probably thinks I'll take him out to his car and fuck his brains out or at the very least suck on his little pin-dick until he gives me a facial. Yeah. That'll happen.

My last turn on the main stage had yielded exactly six pathetic fucking dollars, two each from the dykes and two from him. I'm sure as hell not going to be able to pay my rent with that. Hell, I can barely pay for my discounted drink with that. I don't have much of a choice; I'm going to have to hustle him for lap dances. Well, fuck it, maybe I can charge him double. I down a purple hooter shot and go for it.

I slowly shuffle my 6-inch "fuck me" heels over to where he sits. I come up behind him, lay a finger on his left shoulder and let my long black hair drape over his right shoulder. I peek around and whisper in his ear. "You ready for private dance?" Then I press my fabulous all-original, all-natural D cup tits into his back.

He turns and looks up at me. "Well that depends on how much."

Cheap fucking bastard. If you have to ask, you shouldn't be doing it. "Sixty for two songs," I say.

He looks at me like he's fucking confused. "I thought it was twenty."

Actually it's forty, but I'm trying to squeeze him for whatever I can. I've got rent to pay. "It's sixty."

"I'll give you forty"

"You don't think I'm worth sixty?"

He looks me up and down. "I guess."

You guess? Fuck you. "Let's go then." I turn and walk toward the private booths. Normally I would take his hand and lead him, but tonight I am not in the fucking mood.

Two Very Different Dances

****

He hands me forty dollars probably thinking I would just take it. He's right. I need the bucks and I don't feel like arguing; I just want it to be over. We go into the first in the row of the "private" booths. The booths aren't really all that private since there are no doors - just three red vinyl covered walls and a pink crushed velvet loveseat. We sit next to each other and wait for the song to end. On those rare occasions when I am actually into it, I might strip down while the song finishes, give him the two full songs totally naked then either dress during song four or press him for another set of dances. This is definitely not one of those rare occasions. I am going to strip slowly during his first song and dress toward the end of the second. Management discourages that practice but oh well.

There is an awkward silence between us. Well, awkward for him probably. Me? I don't give a shit; the less spoken the better. Sometimes I make some friendly, meaningless chitchat, where are you from, have you ever been here before, that kind of thing. Tonight, with this guy, I just can't bring myself to do it. This jackass won't be able to handle the silence much longer. Any second now he's going to say something lame. Let's count shall we? One fucking pervert... two fucking perverts... three fucking perverts...

"How long have you been working here?" he asks.

Uh huh. Three fucking perverts. "It's my first week," I lie without looking at him. They love it if they think you're brand new. But that's not why I told him that. I don't want people to know I've pissed away three years of my life dancing naked for assholes instead of doing something worthwhile like teaching or nursing.

"No shit? I could have sworn I've seen you in here before."

"Did you not just hear me say it's my first week?" He responds by raising an eyebrow. God, I am such a bitch.

The song comes to a close and the next one starts up. It's *Friends in Low Places* by Garth Brooks. I can only roll my eyes in disgust. I hate dancing to country. Country songs are rare in strip clubs but once in a while a girl on the main stage (the one who gets to choose the music the DJ plays while she dances up there) likes to do a cowgirl act and she inevitably selects Garth Brooks and probably *Sin Wagon* by the Dixie Chicks to dance to. I'm not a fan of the Chick's music but I have a lot of respect for them after what they said about President Bush. You go girls! The crowd usually digs the country stuff, though – this is Albuquerque, after all. When I get to choose, it's either Pantera or White Zombie.

I stand in front of him and slowly remove my bikini – I shed the top first then turn around and drop the bottoms. In my mind, there's nothing sexy about the way I do it; it's just business. He has one of those creepy smiles on his face; the one they all get when they're feeling superior at the notion that the naked woman in front of them is there purely for their pleasure. It's the smile I've seen a million times on a million pervert losers.

I squeeze in between his legs and force them apart. Thank God it's so dark in here because it's easier to hide the look of disgust on my face when I realize he's wearing satin sweatpants. That is a sure sign that he is going to try to get off during a lap dance. My guess is he isn't wearing any underwear either. I turn, stick my ass on his lap and move it around in a circular motion. I can feel his hard cock as it slips between my cheeks. Ugh, that's so gross. And wow, it must be all of a whopping three inches. I'm sure you make your mama proud. And yup, I was right, no underwear. Do these fucking guys really think we like to be only a thin piece of cloth away their nasty-ass junk?

With any luck I'll leave a skid mark on his nice, white, shiny sweats. Ten minutes before I approached him, I pooped out what seemed like the equivalent of an entire garden hose and used up the last of the toilet paper of the stall I was in. Truth be told, I would have liked to have used a little more. I'm really grinding this guy now. I want to get that tiny prick as far up my ass as possible to get that last little bit of peanut butter I couldn't get in the stall.

Oh that's better. I feel cleaner now. I stand up and turn around to give him a view of the good stuff - The D's and the snatch. I don't want to keep grinding him because he might just cum in his pants and I definitely don't want to give him that kind of satisfaction. I push my tits together and stick them an inch from his face. Touching of any kind is against the rules so all he can do is dream he's got access to goods like this.

Suddenly I feel him grab my ass and squeeze tight. Are you fucking kidding me? I shake myself loose and jump back to the edge of the booth. "No touching! Touch me again and I'll have you arrested!"

He throws his hands up as if I've pointed a gun at him. The expression on his face is half smirk, half surprise. "Whoa, sorry. I didn't know."

Bullshit. They know. They always fucking know. He's trying to get away with some shit and it ain't gonna fly. "Sit on your hands right now."

"Oh come on. I'll be good, I promise."

Sure you will, liar. "What did I just say?"

"Okay, okay, Jesus." He sits on his hands. *Friends in Low Places* fades into *Sin Wagon*. I step in close and lift one of my long sexy legs up and rest it on his shoulder. I give him the obligatory up close look at my spread, bald pussy. Jesus, there's that creepy look again.

I pull my leg back down. I decide to have a little fun and whisper some Italian in his ear. I only know three phrases but believe me, they are so worth it. I get a lot of satisfaction when I get to practice saying them. *"Lei e un che il disgustando maiale,"* I whisper in my huskiest, sexiest voice. He moans his pleasure. He must like it and not realize I just called him a disgusting pig. I'll press on with another. *"Lei me fa i malati."* Yes! Another moan. And I don't think it's because I just told him he makes me sick. I'm going in for the kill. This one is my favorite and sounds the sexiest of the three. *"Spero che le sue palle prendono cancro,"* I say.

"Oh that is so hot!" he whispers back.

He's enjoying the moment as much as I am. I can hardly keep from busting out laughing whenever a guy smiles in ecstasy right after I tell him I hope his balls get cancer.

I squeeze my tits together and once again, place them within an inch of his face. Holy fucking shit! He did *not* just do that! That motherfucker just had the nuts to jam one of his nasty fingers up my pussy. In three years of dancing I have never had that happen. I've never even *heard* of it happening. I react by punching him as hard as I can in the throat; probably not the best choice but fuck it, he was way out of line. He falls back, grabs his throat and gasps for air. "What did I tell you?" I scream. You don't *ever* fucking touch me!"

He responds with a couple of weak coughs. I draw back and sock him in the mouth then grab my clothes and storm off. He just sits there holding his throat with one hand and his mouth with the other. I honestly hope I crushed his windpipe and knocked out some teeth. Un-fucking-believable

I go to the dressing room, slip on my street clothes and gather up the rest of my things. Even though management frowns upon us beating up the customers, my job is probably not in danger. They don't like it when customers pull that kind of shit any more than we do. Even so, that was the last straw; this will be my last night doing this kind of work. I've been thinking about quitting for a while and I'm pretty sure that there probably won't be a better time than right now. I had intended to only dance for a couple of months until I could get some bills paid off. But here it is, three years later and all that's happened is that I got used to having a lot of money and living a more expensive life. I still basically live paycheck to paycheck, so to speak so it hasn't really been worth it. Well you know what? Fuck it, I'm over it. Maybe I'll go stay with my brother out in California for a while, figure out what my next move is.

Whatever that move is I need to make it quick since I'm a little worried about the repercussions of attacking pin-dick back there. I wouldn't be surprised if he went crying to the police about it. Then I'm sure he'll try to sue me for like a million dollars. There is no way I'm going to let that happen. I hear a commotion coming from the main room. It sounds like tables and chairs falling over. I'm sure it has to do with me but I'm not sticking around to find out. So long Booty's, can't say as I'll miss you. I bail out the back door and I'm gone. My new life, for better or worse, starts right now.

****

Vinny Smith

His Dance

I love coming down here on Tuesday nights. You get two lap dances for the price of one and when it's really dead, like tonight, you can usually talk the girls down to about twenty bucks - about half what they normally charge. It's especially true toward the end of the month when rent is due. There are a couple of girls here that kind of dig me; bummer I don't see any of them tonight. That's okay though because that hot brunette at the bar has been checking me out since she was up on stage. Now I'm glad I gave her a buck not only when she took off her top but when she lost the bottoms too. Man, would I love to fuck the shit out of that, or at the very least get her out to the car and let her slob my knob. I would so give her the gift of pearls - all over her face. Yeah baby! Oh, here she comes. Be cool. Act like you couldn't care less.

She asks me if I'm ready for a private dance. I can feel her tits in my back. Those things are so fake.

I look up and ask her how much though I already know. It's been forty bucks since the dawn of time.

"Sixty for two songs," she says.

Sixty? Since when? I'm confused. "I'll give you forty," I say. This bitch is trying to rip me off.

"You don't think I'm worth sixty?"

You know what? She's hot but no stripper is worth sixty. I might, and this is a big might, pay sixty to that tight little hottie, Wendy, in the church youth choir. Come to think of it, it's my choir, I'm the youth pastor for Christ sake - I shouldn't have to pay little Wendy a thing. I look this one up and down. "Yeah, I guess," I say to the sixty dollar question.

"Let's go then." What the hell was that? She's just walking away. She's supposed to take my hand and lead me over there. There is no way I'm giving her more than forty.

****

I follow her back to the private booths and watch her perfect ass sway the whole way. I hand her forty bucks because I'm willing to bet she'll just take it and shut up about it. She doesn't bring up the sixty again so I guess we're all good. We sit down on the little couch in the booth but she just sits there and doesn't say anything. What a cold fish. I hate it when they don't talk. She better step it up or I'm going to have to go have a chat with the manager.

"How long have you been working here?" I ask.

"It's my first week?"

I hate it when they lie like that. She's been here a long time. I'm going to call her on it. "No shit? I could have sworn I've seen you in here before."

"Did you not just hear me say it's my first week? She says. Man, what a bitch. Oh good, finally the song is over. Maybe now we'll get down to business. Yes, it's Garth Brooks. That's a nice change. I hate it when they play all that rap and metal crap.

She finally gets up and stands in front of me. I'm not sure it's possible for this girl to move any slower. Doesn't she realize that it's her job to shake her goods and make me feel like a king? I'm definitely going to have to talk to the manager. She loses her top then turns around and drops the bottoms. I hate when they do that. I'm paying to see her pussy. Ass I can see on any cable channel.

She squeezes between my legs and forcefully spreads them apart. I resist just because I can. I'm going to make her work for that forty bucks. She sits down on my lap and starts moving her ass around. My dick slips nicely between her cheeks. A friend of mine told me about this thing he does where he comes in wearing satin sweats with no underwear. He says if you can get the girl to grind on you during a lap dance, it'll probably be enough to blow a wad right then and there. Of course, now you've made a mess in your pants but it's so dark in these places, probably no one will notice. I'll have to see, I'm trying it for the first time tonight. Shouldn't be too tough, I've already got a *huge* boner and she's really working it. That's more like it. Now I'm getting my money's worth.

I'm just about to cum when she stands and turns around. I've been waiting patiently to get a close up look at her beaver but she could have waited another couple of seconds until I blew my load. She pushes her tits together and sticks them right under my nose. That's nice honey; you want me to get a whiff of that cheap perfume or what? Be careful, you don't want to pop those titties and get goop all over the place.

I reach around and grab a heaping helping of her ass because I just can't help myself. Her skin is so soft and her ass so firm I don't ever want to let go. Then all of a sudden, holy good God, you would think I killed her dog. She jumps back and starts yelling at me. "No touching! Touch me again and I'll have you arrested!"

Her reaction is funny to me but I stifle a laugh and throw my hands up in defeat. "Whoa, sorry. I didn't know." I knew, I just thought I'd see if I could get away with it. You know, so I could get my money's worth.

"Sit on your hands right now."

"Oh come on. I'll be good, I promise." Maybe.

"What did I just say?"

"Okay, okay, Jesus." I go ahead and sit on my hands though I can't guarantee for how long. Nice. It's a Dixie Chicks song. I still like them even though they did disrespect our President. That was so not cool.

Thank God she's calmed down now. She steps back in then sticks her leg up on my shoulder. Now I'm getting the view I paid for. If there was some decent light in here I bet I could look right up into that sloppy gash. She keeps it there for a moment then retreats but then she leans over and whispers something in my ear. It sounds like Spanish and whatever it is, it sure sounds hot. I think I even let out an involuntary moan. I'm pretty sure somewhere in there I heard the Spanish word for stud.

She's smiling. She leans in and whispers something different this time. It sounds like she's saying "lay me, malati." I moan again. I think malati is Spanish for macho man. Her Spanish is awful but who cares? I am so getting laid tonight.

She whispers again. This time she wants me to "bone her cunt." Her translation is a bit crude but I know what she means. "That is so hot," I say.

She squeezes those big, fake boobies together again so I take the hint and give her a little sample of what she's been begging for: I jam my middle finger straight up into heaven.

Next thing I remember I'm gasping for air and she's screaming, "What did I tell you? You don't fucking touch me!" I want to yell back at this crazy bitch and remind her that she came on to me; that if she didn't want me to touch her she shouldn't have led me on. Instead all I can do is cough and then before I can say or do anything else she punches me again, this time right in the mouth. Great, something doesn't feel right and now I taste blood. I think she knocked some teeth loose. Next thing I know, she's gone.

I take a second to catch my breath then I go looking for a manager. I'm so pissed right now it's hard to think straight. My head is throbbing, I'm coughing like crazy, it's hard to swallow and there's blood all over my shirt. I go to the bar and the bartender takes one look at me and signals to somebody, I can't tell who, I assume it's for the manager. "One of your little whores just went psycho on my ass. Look at what she did to me," I say.

"Someone will be right with you," he says and walks away.

They better be, I spend enough money in this place, I better get some action. All of a sudden, two big, burly half Navajo, half Mexican dudes show up and each grab one of my arms. "Hey, what the..." I say.

"You're out of here. Nobody touches the girls," one of them said.

"Is that what she told you? That is a total lie." These guys are starting to piss me off. They aren't stopping and they aren't responding. They keep dragging me toward the door. This is so not cool. I begin to resist. "Wait! Why aren't you listening? You don't even want to hear my side?"

"Nope," the other one said. "You don't have a side. There's no touching. Period."

What a couple of Nazi's. No second chances, no nothing. "You know what?" I say. "I'm calling the cops. This is bullshit!" I yank one arm free and try to make a break for it. I don't get far. Ape number one still has a good grip on my other arm. I try to run but he swings me around and I feel my arm snap as I slam into two or three empty tables. Ow. Pain. I lie in a crumpled heap trying to figure out what my next move is. Not that I'm really able to move at this point. I'm hurting everywhere.

Unfortunately it looks like the next move is going to be made for me because here come the two ape-Nazi's. "Back off!" I yell. "You people just bought yourselves a lawsuit."

They look at each other and say, "You people?" I probably shouldn't have said that exactly. They each grab an ankle and drag me on my back past a pair of lesbians and a couple of gangbangers, all of whom are laughing. Clearly the threat of a lawsuit doesn't intimidate these people.

It only takes a few seconds for me to end up sprawled out on the cold asphalt of the parking lot. I watch the two apes laugh and joke with each other as they head back into the club. I struggle to my feet. It's not that easy to do considering my broken arm and the extreme pain I'm feeling. I walk to my car and think about how this was hands down the worst time I've ever had at Booty's.

As I sit behind the wheel I pray to my Lord and Savior Jesus Christ. First, I ask that he punish that evil stripper. She can't throw the kind of signals she did and then beat me down when I respond accordingly. Second, I ask for quick healing for my injuries as well as some good pain pills. I'm sure Jesus knows how hard it would be to lead the youth choir on Sunday if I'm in this kind of pain. Third, I ask to get what I deserve in my forthcoming lawsuit against Booty's. Once I own this place, there will be some major changes in personnel believe you me.

Wait, what is that smell? It kind of smells like shit. I open the car door so the light will go on and look around for the source of the odor. I notice there's a brown circular stain in my crotch area. Where in the hell did that come from? Unbelievable. That just really caps off the night.

FROM ECURSE69

The sounds coming from under the covers were animal-like, almost inhuman. If anyone were watching, they might think Chris and Emily were contortionists. There were arms and legs twisted and tangled around each other. The lamp and a few other items had been knocked off the nightstand. Clearly a good time was being had by both of them – at least until the pager went off.

Suddenly the action stopped and Chris popped his sweat-drenched blond head out from under the covers near the foot of the bed. He looked over at the nightstand and then down at the floor. He spotted the pager beeping and buzzing and doing a little spastic dance on the hardwood floor. He reached out for it but couldn't quite get it. He promptly and awkwardly joined the fallen items on the floor.

Emily fought her way through the sheets and emerged with a murderous look on her face. The ends of her thick, raven hair were stuck to her shoulders from the sweat. Even with a look that could kill, she still looked beautiful.

Chris looked at the pager and was not happy. "Shit. Number seven is down again." He stood up, found his pants and pulled them on.

"Excuse me! What did I tell you about this shit?" she screamed.

"You're the computer guru," he said. "You should have fixed it right the first time."

"You did *not* just say that!"

"Time is money, baby. That unit sends out 1,200 e-mails an hour."

That did it. Now she was pissed. She jumped out of bed and began to dress.

"I can't believe I was actually feeling guilty for..."

He cut her off mid-sentence and edged his way to the door. "Can we talk about this later? I really need to get her going."

She picked up one of her shoes and winged it at him. It narrowly missed his head but hit the autographed photo of Bill Gates on the wall next to him. Glass splintered all over Bill's face. "That was so *not* cool!" He yelled.

The second shoe knocked the picture off the wall completely.

The dining room in Chris' house was filled with computer gear. He had ten desktop PC's networked together on fold-up tables that stretched from wall to wall. Each one was diligently doing its duty and sending out the requisite 1,200 or so e-mails an hour. Except for number 7. Chris typed some commands into the keyboard and the wounded number 7 sprang back to life. He caressed its monitor like it was a woman. "That's right, baby, work it for daddy."

He hears Emily stomp down the stairs. He hid behind a monitor as if it would shield him from her wrath. He peeked around the monitor just in time to see her flip him off. "Asshole!" she yelled and stormed out.

The coast was clear. He was free to be cocky; something he would never be in her presence. "Emily, Emily, Emily, you little hotheaded vixen... you'll be back."

Chris spun around in his chair and returned to more important matters. He opened up his laptop to access his e-mail. There was a slew of messages from someone with the user name *E.Curse69*. After all the time and money he'd spent protecting his system from spammers like himself, he was quite surprised to find a bunch of them. "Whoa, now, wait one minute. What's this? The spam-ee spams the spam-er?"

The subject lines caught his attention. Each one alerted him to the availability of a variety of sexual products. There was everything from Viagra-like pills and penis enlargers to nudist vacations and bestiality videos. He found it slightly amusing. "Okay, E.Curse, show me what you got."

He clicked on the one offering *Penis Enlargement in Just Minutes.* The message opened but nothing but white appeared on the screen. He stared at it for a second then looked down at his lap as if an open e-mail would actually enlarge his dick. "Nope, still the same. E.Curse, you suck!" he yelled at the screen.

He deleted all of the *E.Curse* e-mails and clicked on compose.

He was about to send out invitations to his annual birthday bash when suddenly a look of surprise crossed his face. He squinted, leaned to one side and let out a series of short farts. The last one sounded and felt different from the others. His look changed from surprise to disgust. "Oh boy. That was wet." He stood slowly, scrunched up his butt cheeks and inched his way out of the room.

In the ten minutes or so that he was in the bathroom, his network of computers did a strange thing. Number 1 shut itself off for a second then came right back on. As soon as it did, number 2 did the same thing. This went on in order until all ten spam computers and the laptop had gone through the same process. The laptop came back up just as Chris came back into the room. He sat down to compose his invitations. He highlighted Emily's name in the address book. "Okay, baby, don't be mad at the birthday boy.

****

Emily sat down on her bed and powered up her laptop for one last check of her e-mail before bed. She saw there was one from Chris with the words *Birthday Party* in the subject line. She clicked on it and when she read what it said, she burst out laughing. "Way to go, dumbass. Way to go." She shut the laptop, turned off the light and went to sleep with a huge smile on her face.

****

The next morning, while Chris was standing in line at his favorite coffee house, he decided to call Emily to see if she had cooled down at all but he could tell by her tone that he had not let enough time pass. "Hey, baby, you still mad?" he asked.

From that point on he never got another word in. Her voice was so loud he had to pull the phone away from his ear. Now practically the whole coffee house could hear her yell at him – and it was not pretty. Every other word was either fuck, fucker, fucking or fucked.

He let her cuss on while he placed his order. "Yeah, I'll have a grande, decaf, skinny, double-whip, no foam, sugar-free, extra-hot, vanilla latte with a single squirt of chocolate, a pinch of cinnamon, double-cupped with no lid." He said all in one breath.

Emily mixed in a few shits and Goddamns. It took him by surprise when she threw in cunt. He looked at the phone then looked up. The entire coffee house had gone silent and everyone was looking at him. He clicked off the phone. "Wrong number," he said.

Rachel, the barista, was just putting the finishing touches on Chris' drink when he arrived at the pick-up side of the counter. "Hey, Rach, you got the invitation to my birthday party, right?"

She looked over at him with fire in her eyes then promptly threw his drink in his face. He screamed out in pain as his ridiculous latte scalded his face. "What the fuck do you think?" she screamed as she yanked off her apron and threw it in his face as well. She stormed out, knocking over anyone in her path.

****

Chris sat on the edge of the ambulance while the paramedics tended to his facial burns. As they were finishing, two of Chris' best friends, Mike and Bryan, walked by laughing and joking. When they saw Chris they pretended like they didn't know him and walked on past. Chris was perplexed. He waved off the rest of the medical attention and chased after them.

"Hey, what's up? Why didn't you stop?" Chris asked.

"You hear something?" Mike said to Bryan

"Kinda sounded like a talking asshole," Bryan responded.

Mike sniffed at the air. "Kinda smells like one too."

"What is up everyone's ass today?" Chris asked. "I don't get it."

Mike and Bryan finally stop to confront him. "Oh, did you send everyone a Nasty-Gram today?" Bryan asked.

"A what?"

"I swear to God if I had any idea you felt that way..." Mike said. He drew his fist back and made like he was going to pop Chris in the mouth. Chris flinched. "... I might have knocked you out a long time ago!"

"What the hell are you talking about?"

Bryan grabbed him by the shirt and pulled him threateningly close. "Next time you decide to send out something like that, you'd better think again!"

Bryan released Chris' shirt and shoved him away. Mike and Bryan started to walk away. "And forget about poker night, you're out of the game."

Chris was stunned. "Oh come on! What did I do?"

****

Once back in the house, Chris flopped down on his couch perplexed, exhausted and in pain – and it wasn't even noon yet. He closed his eyes and quickly drifted off to sleep. It didn't last long though, as he was awakened by the sound of a vehicle screeching to a stop in front of his house. He went to the window and saw his dad get out of his pick-up truck in a rage and throw down the tailgate. Chris went out to greet him.

By the time he reached the truck his dad had already violently tossed several items onto the lawn. Chris looked at the items in horror. They were all his childhood possessions, baby photos and mementos. His mom just sat in the front seat and cried.

"Dad! What the hell?" Chris cried.

His dad continued to empty the truck as he yelled his explanation. "From now on, don't write, don't call, and if I ever see another one of your e-mails, I swear I'll kick your scrawny, little ass!"

"Why? What did I do?"

"You broke your poor mother's heart, that's what you did. Look at her..."

He did. She was crying harder and louder.

"I never thought anyone could be that cruel," his dad said as he slammed the tailgate shut.

His mom finally chimed in. "You're dead to us! We have no son!"

"Mom!"

His dad started the truck then leaned over to address Chris through the passenger side window. "Oh, by the way, we've taken you out of the will. We're leaving everything to the cat."

Dad burned rubber down the street. Chris followed him for a moment but finally gave up and dropped to his knees in the middle of the street. "Noooooooo!"

****

It was after midnight when Chris was finally able to find a comfortable enough position to sleep in. He drifted off to sleep after two hours of trying.

He had been asleep for less than two minutes when he heard a nasty crash from somewhere downstairs. He lay there frozen in fear. The crash was quickly followed by the sound of multiple sets of footsteps ascending his stairs. The bedroom door flew off its hinges and he suddenly had a dozen masked men with FBI jackets in his room. They yanked him out of bed by his ankles. He landed on the hard floor, flat on his back with eleven shotguns pointed at his head.

"Christopher Duval, you're under arrest under federal statute 994223.467," said one of the FBI guys.

"What's that?" Chris asked, voice trembling.

"Federal fucking scumbag charges, that's what, you piece of shit," one particularly pissed off agent screamed.

"What?"

"Federal obscenity charges," said the first guy.

Chris sat straight up. "No fucking way! For what?"

The pissed off agent put his jackbooted foot on Chris' forehead and shoved it back to the floor. "And resisting arrest," he said.

****

,

Three hours later he was still in the interrogation room of the local FBI office. He could see Emily through one of the three windows. She was talking to an agent and shaking her head in disgust. They both turned and looked at him with contempt at the same time.

Emily and the agent shook hands and the agent walked over to the interrogation room and unlocked the door. "Let's go, you've been sprung," the agent said and pointed back at Emily. "Why that sweet girl wants to bail out a piece of shit like you is beyond me."

****

Chris stood at the entrance of his computer room and looked around in shock. It had been cleaned out. Every little piece of equipment had been confiscated by the feds. There was nothing left but a tangled mess of wires.

Emily pulled out her laptop and set it up on Chris' empty desk. She logged on to his e-mail account. "Okay, here's the deal," she said. "You've got yourself a nasty little virus. It's infected your email and your entire network. See, watch this."

Chris looked at the screen over her shoulder.

"I type in *I love you, Chris* and send it back to you..."

She clicked on send. "Now watch what happens."

A second later, the message hit his mailbox. She opened the message which now says, *Fuck you, cocksucker.*

Chris' jaw hit the floor. "Oh my God! It changed everything I sent? How did this happen?"   .

"Have you opened any dubious e-mails lately?"

"No... Wait! Maybe. There was one... something like ecurse69 or something."

"And that didn't seem strange to you?"

Chris didn't answer, he just looked at her with confusion.

"It's an e-curse," she said. "As in electronic curse or e-mail curse. It even says so right in the name. I mean, I don't see how you could miss something like that?"

"Jesus Christ! How do I get rid of it?"

Emily logged off, closed the laptop and headed for the door. "These things usually only have a lifespan of a couple of days. It'll probably be gone by tomorrow or the next day."

"Great, thanks. You're the best," he said.

She opened the front door but turned and looked at him. She had one final thought. "You know, this kind of thing probably wouldn't happen if you spent less time letting your precious computers turn your brain to mush and a little more time on more important things."

"Like what?" he said, as he pulled his cell phone off his belt.

"Like people... loved ones. You remember them don't you?"

He didn't answer. He was preoccupied with his phone list.

"What are you doing?" she asked, suddenly annoyed again. "Did you hear what I said?"

"Yeah – loved ones – I got it." He punched in some numbers. " I gotta get some new machines in here pronto."

"Unbelievable!" She stormed out and slammed the door.

He flinched. "What? Geez."

****

The walls of Emily's den are covered with defiled photos of Chris. There's even a Chris voodoo doll on the desk next to her computer. She sat at the desk and tapped away on her keyboard.

"Okay, you weak little man, here's something you can't resist." A box popped up on her screen that asked her to choose a username. She scrolled down through several choices and chose the one right under *E.Curse69* that said *E.Grief88*.

****

A brand new group of networked computers sat in place of the old ones. They had all booted up and were ready to go. Chris sat in front of a brand new laptop and opened his e-mail. "Okay, let's see what you've got for daddy."

There are several new messages from *E.Grief88*. "Whoa, what have we here? Grief. That's an odd name."

He clicked on the message with *Seducing Lesbians in Five Easy Steps* in the subject line. The message opened but nothing but white appeared on the screen. "Huh. That's weird," he said, perplexed.

A second later the screen went black.

TRINITY SPOILED

I live in a place like no other I've ever been to in the United States - Venice, California, a part of the greater Los Angeles area. One of the things that make Venice unique is the layout of its neighborhoods. There are traditional streets with houses and lawns and sidewalks where you can park your car on the street right in front of your house. There is the canal section where the homes are separated not by a street, but actual canals. The city was named because of this section and its similarity to the original Venice in Italy. Then there are the walk streets with their close proximity to the beach. My girlfriend, Gina and I live in a great little two bedroom house on one of those streets. The nature and layout of the neighborhood are the reasons there is a story to tell. Sort of.

The walk streets are great unless you are into privacy or at the very least, peace and quiet. The streets are lined with single-family homes, duplexes and apartment buildings just like any other street in America. The difference here is that there are no actual streets separating the homes – only sidewalks. Alleys run behind the dwellings and give you access to some very limited random parking and your garage, if you're lucky enough to have one. Most have small front yards where people tend to congregate. Only about eight feet of sidewalk separates our yard from the one directly across from us and there is maybe six feet between each building. It's people living on top of people.

There are some great things about the area. Top of the list is the proximity to the beach. In all likelihood it is probably the most polluted beach in California, but hey, I step out my door and my toes are in the sand in thirty seconds. I also like that the rent is generally cheaper here than in any other beach community in Los Angeles.

Some of the things I like are the same things I hate about it. The fact that your neighbors are so close to each other means that you all know each other and can kind of look out for each others property and such. That I like. When I can hear my neighbor next door taking it out on his toilet after he's just gotten food poisoning for the third time in as many months – that I don't.

Sometimes I like when I can hear my neighbors on the other side having sex. That kind of gets Gina and me in the mood. When they do it at two in the morning and I have to get up at four – again, not liking that. Sometimes it's like a block party around here. People hang around outside and socialize a lot. Sometimes they'll even travel from yard to yard up and down the block. That's all well and good – when I'm not on the verge of having a threesome with Gina and her semi-drunk and horny friend, Carrie.

It was a Saturday evening and I had just gotten home from a particularly difficult day of work. All I wanted to do was have a beer, order a pizza and chill out on the couch but as soon as I stepped into the house, I knew that my evening would not go as planned. Carrie was there and she and Gina had apparently been drinking for several hours already. *Their* plan was to barbeque something and hang outside since it was yet another perfect southern California summer evening.

The reason for Carrie's visits is almost always the same - to lament the fact that doesn't have a man in her life. I've explained at great length to Gina why she doesn't but she always tells me to shut the fuck up. I will tell you, though, since you haven't heard it yet.

First let me say that it's not because she's 40. She's a good-looking woman who looks young for her age and doesn't have anything sagging (I'll tell you why I know that in a minute). Anyway, the first problem is that she gets high and drinks too much. That's probably not going to bother a guy on the first couple of dates since their main interest is to get her in the sack and booze and pot usually will help move that process along. If a relationship does develop, however, those things will likely move along its destruction as well.

The second problem is that she's way too desperate to be in a relationship. I don't know of anyone who will stick around too long when the subject of marriage and kids comes up on the first date. She's also too bossy. She drove her last boyfriend away by telling him everything from how to dress to how to hold his fork when he eats.

The last thing is that she's a whore. I don't mean for a living, I mean for fun. Three boyfriends ago, (I've only known this woman a year, that ought to tell you something) she initiated that old off-limits conversation, about how many sex partners he'd had in the past. He said four: two different girls in high school, his ex-wife and the woman he'd met that became the reason he had an ex-wife.

She was expecting a higher number since guys always seem to inflate it. Her plan was to blast him for being a man-slut and make him feel so guilty that he would do anything and everything to get back on her good side. Not only was that something she could milk for days but it would help to deflect the question off of her. Of course she had no intention of answering it regardless.

He refused to let her off that easy. He really wanted to know. At least he thought he did figuring that at most, her number was probably about 20. She kept refusing to tell him, he finally got pissed and was halfway out the door before Carrie, horny as hell and wanting him to fuck the shit out of her that night blurted out a number. She had thought about it quickly - a little too quickly. She had wanted to be truthful but not too truthful. The number she gave him was about half the actual number. When she blurted out eighty his knees went weak and had to use the wall for support. She quickly realized that she probably should have cut her number by a lot more than half. Eighty sex partners were way too much for most guys to handle. They fought about it and he bailed on her a week later.

Initially Gina and I thought it was because he couldn't handle the high number but when I ran into him at Hooters a month later I found out the real reason he was pissed. Apparently in the month they had dated, they never had sex and it blew his mind that he had not been able to get into the pants of someone who had slept with eighty guys. It never crossed his mind that her number might be double that, (the actual number was 162) and I didn't have the heart to tell him. He also had not realized that the reason she told him anything at all was because she wanted him bad that night and he was actually, finally, going to get the chance. I never told Gina the real reason. I wanted to still be able to refer to Carrie as a whore when I felt like it.

Anyway, back to *my* story. I wasn't in the mood to argue about not doing what I wanted to do and their plan to barbecue didn't sound half bad so I just popped open a beer and went with the flow. We had some good sexual innuendo-filled conversation, some vintage rock music playing and there was a nice cool breeze blowing in off the ocean. It was actually quite nice.

It was nice at least until I looked up and saw the two people I least wanted to see in the world - Joe and Joanne - leave Tom and Jessica's yard six houses down and head toward ours. Joe and Joanne, an older couple, had been friends of Gina's, before they moved off the block, a few months before I moved in. Sometimes it seems like they never left because they are in the neighborhood nearly every weekend (except when Joanne's sick, or at least thinks she is) visiting with everyone whether they were invited or not. Joanne is on more than a dozen medications, for what, no one including Joe knows and many days she can't (or won't) get out bed. Each med probably either cancels out the other or causes a worse illness. I'm pretty sure she'd feel a lot better if she just quit them altogether. Then again, I've also suggested to Gina that maybe Joanne should take a whole bunch of them and mix in heavy amounts of alcohol just to see what happens. Again, Gina just told me to shut the fuck up.

Joanne will call Gina three or four times on any given day and leave rambling messages about nothing and say, "Call me right back, I absolutely *have* to talk to you today." Then when Gina does, she'll get a message saying that their mailbox is full and to try again later. Then several days later Joanne will call again and with her extremely whiny voice and accuse Gina of never calling her back.

Joe and Joanne, of course, blame me for that as well as the fact that they get to spend far less time with Gina ever since I entered the picture. While that is true, I don't dictate who Gina spends her time with. As it happens, not only do they annoy her too but she would rather spend her weekend time with me instead of them anyway. Imagine that. I don't think it ever occurred to them that the reason they don't see Gina as much anymore is because they are not on the block 24/7 like they used be.

So here they were, coming up the street, Joanne waving and Joe smoking a big-ass cigar and both wearing a couple of cheesy smiles. I could feel the beer in my stomach begin to bubble. "Hi," they called from half a block away. Yelling wasn't necessary, we saw them, they saw us and there was no escape. Gina waved back; Carrie and I just smiled and said nothing.

They arrived at the gate and didn't wait for an invitation; they opened it and came right into the yard. Gina and Carrie greeted them with hugs. I didn't even bother to stand. "Well, well, well, look who's actually out of the house," Joe said. "It's nice to see *he* finally let you out of the sack," He said laughing and looking right at me.

"You know it, Joe," I said annoyed. One sentence and these people were already on my last nerve.

Gina giggled and playfully slapped Joe. "Oh you stop it," she said. Carrie and I just looked at each other.

"Apparently she'd rather have sex with him than hang out with us," Joanne whined to Joe. "It's sure not like the old days but whatever."

They never referred to me by my name; it was either "him" or "your boyfriend."

"At least somebody's getting some around here," Carrie said. Her comment went ignored by everyone.

"So what are you guys doing tonight?" I asked, trying to get a feel for how long these idiots would be staying.

"Well we were hoping you guys would join us for sushi at the place around the corner, but obviously that's not going to happen," said Joanne nodding toward our smoking barbecue.

"You're welcome to join us," Gina said. "We only have the three steaks but we don't mind sharing."

The fuck I don't, I exclaimed to myself. Gina paid close to fifteen bucks each for those steaks.

"Doesn't look like your boyfriend here can afford to give up any food. Next strong wind, he might just blow away," Joe said. He always disguised his insults with what he thought was a joke. He was being a complete asshole. He was basically calling me fat since I'm a big guy with a bit of a gut and I'm definitely not blowing away.

Suddenly, Carrie did something surprising – she stuck her hand down my shirt and started rubbing my chest. "Did somebody say blow?" Carrie said.

"Whoa, hey, okay!" Joe said. "We wouldn't want to interrupt that."

Gina saw what Carrie was doing with her hand but didn't say a thing so I just let her keep doing it.

"Let's go, Joe. Gina doesn't have time for us tonight." Or any other night either, I thought.

"That's not true," Gina said. "I totally want to hang out with you guys, we've just been busy that's all."

Joe and Joanne said they understood even though I knew they really didn't. They finally said their goodbyes and headed off to the sushi place. I'm sure they badmouthed me the whole time but I really couldn't care less. Gina and Carrie refreshed their drinks and over dinner we discussed everything but Joe and Joanne.

We watched the sunset from the yard, ate our steaks and then grilled some bananas for dessert. It was an idea Gina had seen on the *Food Network* and they were delicious. Carrie, of course, could not resist teasing me by practicing her blow-job skills on a banana while we waited for the grill to heat up again.

As the evening went on Gina and Carrie got drunker and the dirty dancing with each other began. Gina has a great set of tits and Carrie was all over them, squeezing them both through her shirt and under it. I was a little surprised because that was not like Gina at all; she's the most hetero person I've ever known. There was a constant flow of neighbors and surfers walking by who would yell out an occasional "yeah!" or "woo hoo!" It didn't seem to bother the girls much; they apparently liked the attention. It didn't bother me too much both because I had a front row seat and because Gina wasn't exposing a lot of her body to the public. Besides, my dick had been hard as hell since it all began so there was just no need to put a stop to it. But best of all, there had been no sign of Joe and Joanne in quite a while and frankly, I think we all just forgot about them.

As Gina continued to sway and dance to the music her sweats lowered more and more from her waist and before long, her black thong was in full view. That made me a little uncomfortable but then it suddenly struck me that if we moved our little party inside, there might be a chance of more clothes coming off - maybe both Gina's and Carrie's and believe me, I didn't want to miss that.

Without much prodding I was able to usher them both inside. I saw that their drinks were getting low so I took it upon myself to go to the kitchen and get them both nice, strong refreshments. I handed them the drinks but they just set them on the coffee table and turned their attention to me. Gina shoved me down into a chair and proceeded to give me a lap dance. Carrie helped Gina liberate her fabulous tits from the confinement of a shirt and bra. This was turning into the best lap dance I'd ever had. It was about then that I realized that the front door and the huge windows in our living room were all wide open and that anybody on the sidewalk could see right in.

I slowly worked my way out of the chair. Gina questioned my motives and they both laughed when I told them I had seen a few people crane their necks to see in and it was kind of annoying. The other thing that was kind of on my nerves by then was the volume of the music. It was fine while we were outside but we had not turned it down when we moved inside. I turned it down quite a bit and the girls accused me of being an old curmudgeon. Whatever.

While I was going around "oldifying" the place, Carrie also removed her bra but without removing her top and went back to dirty dancing and feeling up Gina. "I'm not gay but Goddamn, can you believe these things?" Carrie said over and over, referring to Gina's tits. "You are so lucky," she said to me.

"I know," I said as I worked my way into their dance. Damn, Gina looked great in nothing but that thong. We are generally very private with our sex life but at that moment I wanted to fuck her right there, I didn't care who was there.

About that time, Carrie excused herself to the bathroom and Gina sat down on the couch and sucked down her drink. I sat down next to her and we began to kiss. She was unusually frisky. She ran a hand up my shorts and grabbed onto my still rock-hard cock. "You're leaking," she said smiling.

"I'm ready to explode. I want you so fucking bad," I said. I slipped my hand under the thong and ran my fingers through her pussy hair while we kissed some more.

Carrie came back into the room still dressed but twirling her panties on her finger. She let them fly and squeezed in next to Gina on the couch and in the most surprising move yet, Gina let go of my cock and helped Carrie off with her top. I was impressed that the 40-year-old titties were so perky. Her nipples were sticking straight out and were quite large. Gina and I consider cheating to be wrong and

155

totally off-limits. I wasn't quite sure what to do; I hadn't read the rule book on this kind of thing. Was it cheating if it was consensual between all three? I wasn't sure how what was happening fit in with what we believe but I was willing to go with the flow.

Gina and I resumed kissing while Carrie leaned in and began sucking on one of Gina's nipples. I could feel Carrie's fingers sliding up my inner thigh and under a leg of my shorts. She took hold of my cock which was really beginning to feel confined and uncomfortable. Gina's eyes had been closed for most of the encounter so far so I couldn't tell whether she knew that her friend was fondling me or not. Maybe that was okay; I still didn't know was if I was allowed to respond in kind. I decided to test the waters.

I placed my hand just above Carrie's right knee, well under her long skirt, and inched my fingers upward. Gina opened her eyes slowly and first looked at me and then where my hand was. I froze and my eyes opened wide. I feared something bad was about to happen but to my surprise nothing did. Instead, Gina closed her eyes again and slid her tongue into my mouth with even more intensity than before. Okay, I thought, I hope I'm not misinterpreting the signals. Call me crazy but that one seemed to say go.

I kept inching my hand toward the promised land. Much to my delight once I got there I found a soft patch of wet hair. I ran my fingers through it for a minute then slowly slid two fingers deep into her hot pussy. Through the music I could hear her subtle moan of pleasure. I also thought I could hear something much more disturbing: The sound of Joe and Joanne calling Gina's name over and over from the sidewalk like a couple of little fucking kids.

I'm not sure if Gina heard them or was ignoring them or what but right at that moment she unbuttoned and unzipped my shorts. "Why don't we move this to the bedroom," Carrie said.

What a great suggestion! This woman was smart! I withdrew my fingers from Carrie and backed away from Gina. I was not going to impede the progress. I stood up and through a gap in the blinds I could see Joe and Joanne waving at me from the sidewalk. Jesus, what's wrong with these people? Go bother somebody else.

I took Gina's hand and led her down the hallway toward the bedroom. Carrie was right behind us. They better not come knocking on the door, I thought. Take the hint and go home. *Please!*

We made it to the bedroom, out of ear and eyeshot of Joe and Joanne. Gina lay down on her back and I pulled off her thong. Carrie came up behind me and pulled my shorts and boxers down to my ankles and I gladly stepped out of them. Carrie then reached around and again wrapped her fingers around my dick. Gina grabbed the bottom of my shirt and pulled it off over my head. Carrie let go of my cock and Gina spread her legs wide. I crawled in between them like a man crawling through the desert toward the mirage. I felt like I could explode right then.

I lay my dick on Gina's bush and slid it around like a snake in the grass; I usually liked to do that just before I entered her. But this time, instead of her guiding me in as usual, she pushed me off. I hoped the booze wasn't wearing off and she was having second thoughts but then I realized she wasn't pushing me off as much as she was pushing me over onto my back. She did that once in a while when she wanted to be on top. Needless to say, I was fine with that.

I rolled over and saw that Carrie was now completely naked. I was blown away. This 40-year-old woman had the body of someone at least fifteen to twenty years younger. I could now see the whole package, not just the perky tits. Her dark bush was trimmed and shaped not quite in a triangle but more like a baseball home plate - a black, fuzzy home plate that I desperately wanted to slide into. She looked phenomenal.

Gina climbed on top and straddled me. She began to stroke me and rub some of the leakage around until my cock was nice and slippery. Carrie climbed up facing Gina and straddled my chest. She began to wiggle backward, moving her pussy closer and closer to my face. I stuck my tongue out and was millimeters from reaching her clit when I once again heard the horrifying sound of Joe and Joanne calling out Gina's name. Only this time it sounded closer than the street - a lot closer. Then I heard the front door slam. Holy shit! I forgot they had a key! We had given them one so they could feed the fucking cat when we're out of town. The fucking cat we don't even have anymore! These people had the balls to use their fucking key and come right in!

The slamming of the door got everyone's attention. You never saw anybody sober up as fast as Carrie and Gina did at the moment when they heard that door slam.

"Hello," Joanne called out in her grating voice. "Where are you?"

"Just a minute," Gina yelled as we all scrambled for clothes.

"What are you guys doing?" Joe asked.

"Be out in a minute," Gina said.

Clothes flew around the room as the girls ripped through the closet to find something to wear. Half of what Carrie had been wearing and all of what Gina had worn was still scattered all over the living room. It wouldn't take a genius to figure out what we were doing and believe me, Joe and Joanne were not geniuses.

I was the first one dressed but I was not sure I could go out there and deal with them. I was on the verge of exploding but not in the good way I had been before. Gina quickly finished and led the way out of the bedroom. I had always wanted to tell them to fuck off but Gina would never let me. I thought I might finally get my chance.

Joe and Joanne stood in the middle of the living room. Joanne looked concerned. "We were out there calling for you. Why didn't you come out? What are you guys doing back there?"

Before Gina could speak, Joe held up Carrie's panties and examined them. "Whose are these?" he asked in a way that creeped us out.

"Okay, give it here," Gina said, more stern than I'd ever heard.

Joe held out the panties. "Here, sorry."

"Not those!" Gina yelled.

"Yes those!" Carrie screeched, snatching them from Joe's hand.

"I mean the key. Give me your Goddamn key right now," said Gina.

"Why?" they asked in unison.

"Why? You have to ask why? You're intruding in our house, that's why."

"How could we be intruding, we always let ourselves in?" Joanne said.

"When? When we're not here?"

"Sure, whenever we're in the neighborhood."

"Why?"

"Sometimes we just need to get away from Tom and Jessica. They can be a little annoying."

Carrie and I looked at each other with raised eyebrows.

"Why don't you just go home then?"

"It's boring there. We'd rather come over here and hang out."

"Sometimes it's an emergency though, remember?" Joe asked Joanne.

"Emergency?" I asked.

"One time while we were at Tom and Jessica's, Joe had to fart but accidentally went poopies instead so he really needed to borrow some underwear."

"Ewwww," Gina and Carrie groaned at the same time.

"So you sharted then came over here to raid my underwear drawer?" I said, thoroughly disgusted.

Joe laughed, "Oh God no, yours were way too big for me, I had to borrow Gina's," he explained. "What I don't get is how anybody can wear those little thong thingys. Went right up my butt and stayed there the rest of the day."

We were all shocked and had no use for the visual that confession had conjured up. Joe and Joanne just looked at us like they had no idea that there might be a problem with that situation. "All right, that's it. Give up the key and get the fuck out." I said, happy that I was finally getting my chance to yell at them.

They looked at Gina with sad eyes. "Now how do you expect us to feed the cat if we don't have a key?"

"The cat died a year ago! His ashes are right here!" Gina pointed to a small urn on the coffee table.

"Umm... that's not an ashtray?" Joe asked.

"No it's not. Why?" said Gina.

"No reason. Let's go Jo."

"Not without that key," Gina said, firmly.

They reluctantly handed the key over and finally took off, hopefully for the last time. I knew conversations about this would be forthcoming, but at that moment all I wanted to do was get back to where Gina and Carrie and I had left off.

"Well, that was interesting," I said. "I say we get back to what we were doing."

"Actually, that whole thing really tired me out. I think I'll just head for home," Carrie said.

"Oh come on, stay awhile. Let me fix you another drink." I said.

"She said she was tired," Gina said in the stern voice again.

I knew right then that I would be in deep trouble if I pushed it. I thought it best to keep my mouth shut.

****

A year has gone by and Joe and Joanne are thankfully still out of our lives. We had several conversations about them and decided that there was no way we could ever trust them again; they had gone too far with invading our privacy. Speaking of privacy, we have a lot more of it now that we've moved to the Venice canals. It's only five blocks from the beach and we have not given keys to any of our friends or neighbors.

The almost threesome has not been spoken of since. It was one of those strange moments in time that will never happen again and that's fine with me. Gina is and only was the only one I want. Thinking about it now, I'm glad it never happened. The thought that I might have been Carrie's number 163 makes me kind of ill.

Carrie met a guy a few weeks after that night and they really hit it off. They have been together ever since. He became number 165. Gina and I have no idea who numbers 163 and 164 were.

CHEMISTRY

Every square inch of the Ford Explorer was packed with boxes and suitcases. The space between the two front seats was filled with crushed cans of Red Bull and empty bags of beef jerky. Darrin, the smarmy frat boy behind the wheel, was definitely more interested in the sleeping, brunette beauty in the passenger seat than the desert highway in front of him.

It was obvious why. In addition to Amanda being about as near a 10 as one could get, she had just shifted in her seat and her perfect right breast now seemed extremely close to popping out of her too-tight blouse. Was that part of a nipple he was seeing? Why couldn't this happen before the sun went down when there was more light? The boys at the frat house back at Texas Christian were going to want to see this. He reached back behind the seat and fumbled around for a moment before pulling out a small video camera. He alternated between watching the road and getting the camera rolling. He taped her for a few moments before he saw the sign welcoming them to

Arizona. Just beyond that sign was a billboard for the Stateline Motel, exit now. The Red Bull just wasn't doing it and he was looking at seven more hours to L.A. She'd be pissed but fuck it; he wasn't going to risk his life for her. It might be different if she was his girlfriend, but she wasn't, she was someone else's.

He parked in front of the motel office and shut off the Explorer. He took one last stare before shaking her shoulder. "Hey, wake up, we're here."

She slowly opened her eyes and stretched her arms out. She quickly realized her tit was nearly exposed and scrambled to readjust. She looked around and was annoyed at the surroundings. "Here where? This doesn't look like L.A."

"It's not, we're in Arizona," came his casual reply. "We're still seven hours out."

"So why are we stopped then?"

"I'm beat, I can barely keep my eyes open."

"You swore to me you could make it without stopping."

"Yeah," he said with mock concern. "I don't know what I was thinking. Fort Worth to L.A. in one stretch is a long-ass ride."

She turned away and shook her head in disgust. What an asshole. She definitely would have done this a different way if she'd foreseen this new development.

"You're welcome to take over any time," he said, like that was a real option.

Amanda had gotten a DUI eight months prior and lost her license for a year. When she decided she wanted to take a break from school and move back home to California she posted a flyer in the Student Union for someone to drive her and her stuff in her SUV, she'd pay for gas and food. The deal was, though, they had to drive straight through since there was no money in the budget for a motel stopover. Darrin was the only one who answered the ad. After asking around, she found a friend of a friend who knew him and deemed him trustworthy enough to do the job.

So now here they were, in the middle of the desert, in a motel parking lot arguing about something that was not supposed to be an issue. She knew she was at his mercy and she hated it. She wanted to smack the smirk off his face. "I guess the rooms are on your dime then," she said, as she got out of the Explorer. He watched her perfect ass walk into the motel office.

****

Amanda emerged from the motel office restroom just as Darrin was receiving the room keys. She barely noticed him since she was knee-deep in a cell phone conversation with her girlfriend who apparently was not happy about the stopover. "Look, Claire, what do you want me to do? I'll be there tomorrow, it's the best I can do at this point."

Darrin walked up to her and shook the keys in her face. She shot him a look that clearly said, "fuck off" and turned away to finish the conversation. "I have to go, I'll call once we're on the road again."

He made a few obnoxious sexual gestures behind her back then looked over at the redneck desk clerk hoping for a laugh. He got one. She quickly turned around, wondering what the laughter was all about. They immediately stopped. Each received a dirty look before she turned her back to finish her conversation.

"Yes, he knows about us and yes, we have separate rooms."

Darrin looked at the desk clerk again, stuck two fingers in front of his lips and wiggled his tongue between them. The desk clerk raised and eyebrow and smiled. "I love you too," she said, and closed her phone.

"So, I've got good news and bad news," Darrin said. "Good news is we've got a room."

"*A* room? As in *one* room?"

"That's the bad news, they only had one left."

"You have got to be kidding."

"It's cool, though, 'cause the good news is it has two beds."

He held out her key. She stared at him for a moment with hate in her eyes then snatched the key from his hand. "This is so *not* cool."

"Oh relax, I wouldn't think of coming between you and what's-her-name."

"Her name is Claire."

"Whatever."

She was out the door before he could say another word.

Darrin looked at the desk clerk and smiled. "I am such a liar."

****

By the time an hour had gone by, she had calmed down and made him buy her dinner. He had traded in his obnoxious frat boy persona for a gentler, softer side. She wondered why he kept it suppressed. It was quite nice, actually.

They sat on his bed with a vegetarian pizza, a couple of bottles of merlot and a lot of laughter. He was actually a funny guy. Who knew? Just as she sucked down the last drop of wine out of her plastic motel cup, he offered to refill it. She turned it down at first since she felt a little tipsy, but since there was only about a cupful left, it was easy to persuade her to polish it off.

He got off the bed to deposit the bottle in the trash but carelessly flopped back down just as she was about to take another sip. This caused her to spill the wine all over the front of her blouse. He freaked out, quickly grabbed some napkins and without thinking, made a move to dry off her chest. She went from zero to bitch in a flash. She snatched the napkins out of his hand and smacked his arm away. "Keep your fucking hands off?" she screamed. "I'll do it!"

Darrin was genuinely remorseful of the turn the turn of events. "Shit, I'm sorry."

She saw the horrified look on his face and sensed his sincerity. She instantly calmed down. "No, it's okay, I got it." She had done all she could with the napkins so she hopped off the bed and went to her suitcase. She pulled out a bottle that looked like it contained some sort of chemical. It instantly felt light so she held it up for a better look. Sure enough, it was empty. "Shit." She tossed it in the trash. "Gimme the keys, I've got more in the car."

"More what?" he asked.

"Chloroform. It's an awesome stain remover"

"No shit?"

"No shit." She took the keys and went outside.

He found that strange. When she came back in with a fresh bottle, his curiosity got the best of him. "Where did you get that stuff? You can't buy it over the counter can you?"

"No, my dad uses it in his dry clean shops. He gives me all I want."

She disappeared into the bathroom and he began to clean up.

Chemistry

As he gathered up the trash, he happened to glance in the mirror over the dresser. His jaw dropped open and the trash fell out of his arms. While there was a wall separating the bedroom from the bathroom, the mirror was situated in such a way that he could look at it and see right into the bathroom if the door was open – which it was. And there she was, in her bra, at the sink, rubbing the stain away. He sat there frozen, taking it all in.

She held up the blouse to the light to examine the stain. Satisfied with the results, she flipped on the heat lamp and laid the blouse out on the counter. Then, oblivious to the fact that Darrin could see every move, she removed her bra.

He got an instant erection and his heart started to pound rapidly. His breaths now came quick and short. Her tits were absolutely fucking perfect. This was a gift, a gift from God that couldn't possibly get any better. Could it?

As he pondered that thought, she did the unthinkable – she removed her jeans and panties. He stopped breathing altogether. Her pussy was perfect. The hair was trimmed and triangular just the way he liked it. It felt like his dick would rip right through his jeans. Forget Viagra, if they could somehow bottle this...

She reached for a towel, wrapped it around herself and took a step toward the door. Terrified of getting caught, he scrambled to gather up the garbage again. She poked her head around the corner and announced her intention to take a shower.

"Okay," he said, voice cracking. He cleared his throat. "How's the stain?"

"I think it'll be fine."

"Good."

He collapsed on the bed as she shut the door. He lay there for a moment thinking about what he'd just seen. How could she not have seen him watching her? She couldn't possibly have *wanted* him to see. Could she? What if she'd never even been with a guy? Maybe she didn't know what she was missing. Maybe he was the guy to help her figure it out. His mind was racing a mile a minute.

The sound of the shower caught his attention. He stared at the closed door in the mirror for a moment. He got up and tiptoed to the door, even though she never would have heard him anyway. What if he walked in right now? What would she do? Should he try it? He took hold of the doorknob. He took a deep breath and slowly turned it. It was locked. Some distant part of his conscience was relieved. He returned to the bed and cleaned up the trash.

An hour later Amanda put her book down and got up to check on her blouse. Darrin watched her as she walked past and thought that even in ratty sweat pants and oversized t-shirt she was a vision to behold. She tried not to look at him. She was disgusted by the fact that he so casually lay there on top of his bed in his boxers and watched TV. "Why don't you put some clothes on for Christ sake?"

"What are you bitching about, I usually sleep naked."

"Can you at least tighten up or something? You're sprouting out all over."

The pee hole was open enough that he had hair sticking out. He just smirked and did nothing.

"Shit," came the exclamation from the bathroom.

"Shit what?"

"This heat lamp is a piece of shit. This isn't drying at all. I'm going to leave it on for a while."

"What do I care, I don't pay the electric bill around here."

She crawled back into her bed and lay with her back to him. After a few moments the sound of the TV was starting to get on her last nerve. "How long are you going to keep that on? I thought you were tired."

"Just winding down a little. Is it bothering you?"

"Yes."

He promptly turned it off and shut out the light, leaving only the glow from the heat lamp for light.

"Sorry," he said with sincerity. "About the sleepover, I mean."

"Forget it, I'd rather get there safely."

"You sure?"

"Yeah... just stay on your side of the room."

He hesitated for a moment before finally responding, "Yeah... sure."

He laid there for what seemed like an hour and stared at her blanket-covered shape. When he couldn't take it anymore, he slipped his hand into his shorts and started to rub. He was only seconds into it when she coughed. He nearly jumped out of his skin. His heart felt like it would pound its way out of his chest. He scurried out of bed and locked himself in the bathroom. He yanked his shorts down, slapped his hand against the wall for leverage and went to town.

It was over quick and it was quite messy. He got his sticky goo all over the toilet, the wall behind it, part of the tub and God only knows how it got on the mirror. He grabbed a towel and wiped up the mess but in doing so he noticed something. Amanda had left the bottle of chloroform on the sink. He went to pick it up but immediately dropped it into the sink. The bottle was scorching hot from the heat lamp. It made what seemed to him, a deafening sound when it hit the porcelain. It probably would have been worse had it shattered. He cussed out loud and looked at his fingertips that had now turned red. He ran the faucet and cooled both his hand and the bottle. He dried it off with a towel and in the process was struck with a sinister idea. If this shit worked like it did in the movies, it could wind up being an interesting night.

He saturated another towel with the contents of the bottle and quietly left the bathroom. Miraculously, Amanda didn't wake up when Darrin dropped the bottle and was still fast asleep. He thanked God to himself and stood over her with the towel in hand. His heart was pounding again. He held the towel by the corners and inched it closer to her face. He gently placed it over her face and then quickly backed away, hoping for the best. She didn't stir. He watched her closely for signs of consciousness. There weren't any. Then it hit him: How long does it take for this shit to work? It only takes seconds in the movies. And how long does the effect last? They never show that shit in the movies. Why don't they ever show that in the movies? What if there's a delicate chemical balance that has to be adhered to? Why didn't he fucking pay attention in chemistry class? There was no sense in fretting about it now besides, she hadn't moved in a couple of minutes. He slowly removed the towel from her face. He whispered her name. There was no response. He said it louder. Nothing. He nudged her. Still nothing. This was good. The shit actually worked.

He tossed the towel on his bed and flipped on the lights. He pulled back her blankets and rolled her onto her back. Of all the girls he'd fucked, this one was definitely the hottest. Too bad she was going to miss it. He figured at the very least, she'd wake up with a smile on her face. Off came her t-shirt. He discovered she didn't wear a bra to bed. The sight of those perfect tits up close made him instantly hard again. When the sweats came off he was pleased to see she didn't wear panties to bed either. He quickly shed the rest of his clothes.

Without proof, this little adventure would be nothing but an unlikely fish tale to the boys back at the frat house. Out came the video camera. He taped himself sticking his fingers everywhere he could then licking them clean. His cock had never been harder. He couldn't resist the fun of pretending to stick it in her ears and nose. This was going to be a classic video. He was going to be a legend.

After about fifteen minutes he'd had enough of the silly stuff and wanted to get down to business. He set the camera on the dresser, checked the angle and went for it. Over the course of the next thirty-five minutes, fourteen positions were undertaken and to avoid being cruel, he stuck it in her mouth *before* he stuck it in her ass so she wouldn't wake up with nasty breath. He came all over her face and chest then taped close ups of the results. This had been the most exciting experience of Darrin's young life.

****

The next morning, Darrin woke up later than he wanted to. He couldn't believe it was almost noon. He'd slept better than he had since high school. He looked over at Amanda and was pleased with himself for the job he'd done cleaning up the mess and getting her clothes back on. She must have enjoyed it too because she was still asleep as well.

He figured she would be up by the time he got out of the shower. She wasn't. It was time to wake her up. Problem was, she wasn't waking up. He yelled and shook her, to no avail. It didn't take long to realize something was wrong. He started to panic. What the fuck? This shit doesn't happen in the movies. They always wake up.

He listened to her chest and checked for a pulse. He heard and felt nothing. She had seemed softer and warmer before but now she was cool and kind of hard. No, this couldn't be. There was no fucking way she could be dead. People don't die from this shit. Do they? Why the fuck hadn't he paid attention in class? Panic set in and his mind raced. It finally hit home -- she was dead and he might very well be fucked. He went berserk, yelling, screaming and throwing things. He didn't notice that in his rage he had knocked the video camera behind the dresser.

When his fit was over and he had calmed down he paced the room and tried to figure out what to do. A knock at the door made him jump out of his skin. Darrin froze and said nothing. Another knock was followed by the voice of the manager. "Everything okay in there?"

With Darrin's heart in his throat, he managed a weak and squeaky "Yes."

The manager was not convinced. "Can you open the door, please?"

Darrin was paralyzed with fear. "We're not dressed."

"The guests in the room next door said it sounded like a fight going on in there."

"No, nothing going on in here. We're cool. Must've been someone else."

"Sir, if you don't open the door, I'm going to have no choice but to call the sheriff.

Darrin definitely didn't need that kind of action so he gave in and cracked the door open. The manager, a pushy, fat little fuck, surprised Darrin and pushed the door open further than Darrin would have wanted. "Nothing going on, huh? This room is trashed!"

Darrin had to think fast. He stepped in front of the manager's view and pushed him back out the door. "You mind keeping it down? My girlfriend's sleeping."

"Okay, first of all, it's time she got up because checkout time was noon and it's way past that now."

"Look, I'll pay the extra night, okay? Now if there's nothing else..." Darrin attempted to shut the door but the manager blocked it with his foot.

"You expect me to believe she slept through all that racket?"

Darrin was getting pissed. "Look, man, it was last night, we got a little crazy, that's all. I'll clean the fucking room and pay the extra fucking night, okay? Now fuck off!" Darrin stomped on the manager's foot, slammed the door and locked it. "Pushy motherfucker."

Darrin took a deep breath then went into scramble mode. He did a whirlwind job of packing. He dumped the chloroform in the sink, peeled the label off and flushed it. He gathered up the towels. At least two of them were cum-stained, two more had chloroform on them, two had been used for hand towels, two for the shower and since he definitely didn't want to smell-check any of them, he packed them all into a pillowcase then snuck outside with them and the bottle. He smashed the bottle in the dumpster of the pizza place next door and tossed the bag of towels in on top of it. He ran back in to take a quick look around and decided he was ready to go. He grabbed his duffel bag and headed for the door. He took one last look at Amanda as he opened the door. "Sorry about this, wish I could take you with me but, well, you know." He turned to walk out and bumped right into two sheriff's deputies.

"Know, what?" one deputy asked.

The bag dropped out of Darrin's hand, as he stood there stunned.

****

Darrin tapped his fingers anxiously on the interrogation room table. According to the clock on the wall he'd been there four hours. He wasn't sure if the cops were buying his story that Amanda just died in her sleep and it made him really nervous. He had no idea whether or not the chloroform could be detected in her system. He wished he hadn't cheated his way through that Goddamned chemistry class. He couldn't remember a thing about the lecture on chloroform other than there had been one.

The sheriff and another man entered the room, both with disturbed looks on their faces. Here it was, hopefully the moment of truth, except that they just stared at him and said nothing for what seemed like an eternity. He couldn't take it he had to say something. "So? What's the deal?"

"This is Dr. Stein, the coroner, I'll let him explain," said the Sheriff.

"How much do you know about chloroform, son?" said the Doctor.

Darrin's heart dropped down into his colon. He'd gotten rid of the liquid and the bottle. Fuck, it must have been detectible in her system. He tried to remain calm. "Chloroform? What does that have to do with anything? Is that what killed her, because as far as I know we didn't have any..."

"No, chloroform didn't kill her," the Doctor said, cutting Darrin off. "Phosgene did."

"Phosgene? I don't get it. What the fuck is that?"

"Phosgene was used by the Germans in the gas chambers. It's what chloroform turns into when it's exposed to sunlight. It then becomes deadly if it rises above seventy degrees. That's what killed her."

Darrin flashed first on the hot bottle of chloroform in the bathroom then on the smashed bottle in the dumpster. "I'm sorry, I still don't know anything about chloroform."

"Oh really? Recognize this?" The sheriff pulled an empty bottle out of a bag. "It was in the trash can in your room."

Darrin flashed on Amanda tossing out the first bottle and going out to get the second.

"We also found this," the sheriff said, pulling out the video camera.

Darrin turned white and sat back in his chair.

"Tell him about the estimated time of death, Doc," the sheriff said.

"The phosgene likely killed her within minutes of inhalation."

Darrin looked at one then the other, knowing what they were going to say, but hoping they wouldn't.

The sheriff leaned in and got in Darrin's face. "So basically, you sick little fuck, you raped a dead girl."

Darrin began to dry heave.

"I believe the time of death to be around 11 pm, about the same time the timecode on the video begins," the doctor said.

"You'll be going away for a very long time, I guarantee you," the sheriff said.

Darrin slumped over, buried his head in his arms and cried. The sheriff and the doctor headed for the door. The sheriff stopped and turned to Darrin one last time. "I can't believe a good-looking kid like you has to resort to such things just to get laid. What made you do it? Why would you use chloroform on that girl?"

Darrin looked up and wiped his nose on his sleeve. "It was there. It was just fucking there."

FIRST NIGHT BACK

"No thanks, I'm done. It's my first night back," I told the bartender when he asked if I wanted another. Two drinks were enough, all I wanted was to get out of this hell and get back to my motel. It was karaoke night at this little joint in Burbank and the woman I was with wanted to dance. First of all, I hate to dance because I suck at it. Second of all, who can dance when the singing is so God-awful bad? I didn't want to go there at all but it was the only place open late on a Sunday night and I had no place to dump this woman.

Anna and I had been working on a mutual friend's documentary film and had just finished following a *NASCAR* driver all over hell and back for two months. I had given up my apartment to take the job thinking I could save two months rent and get something new when I came back. In the meantime, I was staying in this little motel close to where we'd be editing the film. Anna on the other hand, was from

New York and had only one other friend in L.A., this idiot-girl named Vicky whom I knew from another project and whom she was supposed to be staying with.

Anna had made numerous attempts to reach Vicky throughout the day to no avail. I suggested she get a room for the night but she insisted Vicky was solid and that she would follow through on her promise to put her up. "Let's go get a drink while we wait," she suggested innocently enough. I had given her a ride back from Phoenix and was, unfortunately, her only transportation until idiot-girl picked her up. I couldn't just dump her somewhere, I felt like I needed to at least make sure she met up with her friend. So there I sat, wishing for either a phone call from idiot-girl or a quick death.

Two things I need to mention about Anna. First, she had a husband back in New York and second, she was apparently a raging alcoholic. I'd seen her put away a few while we were on the road and she never went back to her room without a bottle of wine. I never much cared, though, since she always made it to the shoots on time and hadn't made any costly fuck-ups. But now she was on my time and damn, she was really sucking them down. She'd had at least three martinis and four shots of something that smelled pretty fucking nasty. Then when she could hardly stand, much less walk, she tried to drag me out to dance. "Okay, that's it, we're going to have to go," I said when she fell to the floor.

"Oh come on, one more drink," she pleaded.

"I don't think so." I lifted her off the dance floor and pulled her toward the door.

"What about, Vicky? She's supposed to come pick me up."

"I can't wait any longer, I gotta work in the morning," I said.

"So where am I gonna sleep?"

"My room I guess."

"Oh, really. Thinking of making a move, are you?" She was slurring her words and her eyes were barely open. "I wonder what my husband would think about that," she said in a voice loud enough for everyone to hear. They always mentioned their husbands or boyfriends whenever they wanted the other people in the room to know they weren't "with" you.

"I think he'd want to know you were safe," I said. I wished that poor, dumb bastard was there. This should be his problem, not mine. God I hated drunks.

"I'm just fucking with you," she slurred as she tried to slap me playfully upside my head.

"Okay," I said. I caught her arm right before she made contact with my noggin. "Let's just go."

Anna was barely conscious by the time we reached the motel. I carried her from the car to the room and flopped her down on the bed – the only bed. I was going to have to either sleep on the floor or in a chair. First night back and I couldn't even sleep in a bed. It's not that I couldn't, I just didn't want to have to explain an awkward situation in the morning. I was better off elsewhere.

I went to the closet and pulled the extra pillow and blanket off the shelf. I turned around and saw that Anna was now standing next to the bed fiddling with the button on her jeans. "What are you doing?" I asked.

"I have to poop," she said.

That's information I could have done without. "Umm... bathroom's thataway," I said, pointing the correct direction.

"Okay," she said, and dropped her jeans before I could say anything else.

She was wearing a sexy blue thong that looked textbook perfect on her. I couldn't help but stare. I kept quiet so as not to remind her that she was half naked in a motel room with a guy other than her husband. With her eyes barely open, she headed for the exit. "Whoa, hang on, it's this way." I took her by the arm and led her to the bathroom instead.

She opened her eyes and looked around. "Oh, yeah. Thanks."

I left her to her movements and shut the door behind me. I hoped like hell she could take care of everything herself.

I put aside thoughts of what she was doing in there and tried to concentrate on the memory of her in that thong. I forgot to mention before that this was a good-looking girl. She was in her late-twenties, had dark, shoulder-length hair and a killer body. She was a vegan, which explained the killer body but didn't explain the alcohol abuse. She was taking care of herself one way and killing herself in another. As hard as I tried, I couldn't help but think about what would happen if she shit and passed out before she could, you know, wipe.

About ten minutes went by with no noise then suddenly the glorious sound of a toilet flush. Thank God, I thought, but then there was no more noise for a few more minutes. Finally, as I was about to knock on the door, I heard what sounded like flesh hitting the floor. I tried to open the door but she had fallen against it. I pushed it open enough to squeeze in. Apparently she'd passed out as she was leaving. I glanced around and every indication was that she had taken care of business without incident.

I carried her back, laid her on the bed and cursed under my breath. Did I mention I hate drunks? Thong or no thong, I wasn't having fun. That didn't stop me from staring at her a while longer, though.

Suddenly I had a thought. I remembered one night when a bunch of guys on the crew and I were sitting around discussing Anna and the other four women on the project. We were guessing how each one might maintain their pussy hair. Out of the five, only two had been confirmed. Julia had fucked one of the guys in the group so we knew she was shaved bare and Maria was dating, Eddie, who had no qualms in telling us that she had trimmed it down to a little landing strip. Jeannette was a hippie-type so we were pretty confident she had a full, uncontrolled bush. As anal as Jessie was, she just had to keep hers perfectly manicured. The jury was still out on Anna. She was the only one who was married and the only one no one could agree on. Everyone guessed something different. I said she was bare around the lips with a triangular tuft of hair above. Eddie was adamant that she was full bush; Jerry insisted she was shaved and Tommy couldn't decide between mohawk or trimmed and shaped but was leaning toward trimmed and shaped. It was quite the conundrum.

So there I was, standing over the pussy in question with nothing but one thin layer of cloth between me and the answer. I thought I should get something for all this trouble my first night back. I slowly pulled the top of the thong away from her skin and leaned in for a peek. I saw hair but I couldn't see the whole thing. I lifted a little higher for a better look.

"What are you doing?" she whined.

I jumped back and nearly shit my pants. The thong snapped back into place. I was white with fear. "Just take them off, Jeff," she whispered. Her eyes were closed.

Jeff? My name is Nick. Jeff is her husband's name. Whoa, hold on a minute, I thought.

"Make love to me, Jeff."

I suddenly realized how hard my cock was. I was frozen in place.

"Come on, Baby, it's my first night back. Don't you want to fuck?" She rolled onto her side and made a blind grab for my belt buckle. She got a hold of my cock instead. She started to squeeze and pull. That didn't feel too fucking good but I made a snap decision to help her out a little. I moved in close and slid out of my pants in between gropes. Mr. Johnson was now free. Even on the edge of consciousness, she knew exactly what she wanted to do with it. She took it in her mouth and I suddenly had a horrible thought. What if in her drunken stupor she dreamed she was eating a carrot or a banana or, God forbid, a dill pickle, and decided to snap off a chunk. All of a sudden I wasn't feeling too comfortable with my snap decision but I bravely soldiered on anyway.

She slobbered all over it for a few minutes then passed out again with her mouth full of my dick. I guessed that she was done for the night so I pulled out. As soon as I did, she regained consciousness. "Just hurry already," she whined, and rolled onto her back. "Fuck me, goddammit!" She flopped around as she attempted to remove the thong. I stood there and chuckled at the pathetic sight. As soon as they cleared her crotch, I realized that fucking Eddie had been right. Full bush, no question about it. I just knew that once I confirmed it he would gloat and tell us he told us so, ad nauseam.

Anyone else might have helped her out instead of watching her flail about, tangled up in her own underwear, but I have this rule. If they pull their own panties off, they can't complain later that they were coerced or forced or whatever. It's a clear signal that sex will be happening. At least that's how it plays out in my warped little mind. Okay, sure she was drunk, but that's not my fault. She gets that thong off and thinks I'm her husband, I'm getting some. I wondered for a brief moment at what point my morals had escaped the room. I went from being a gentleman and sleeping in a chair to getting a blowjob from some dude's drunk wife in just a couple of minutes. I am so weak.

Finally she got free of her encumbrance. She didn't waste any time, she laid there with her eyes closed and spread her long, sexy legs. "Eat me, motherfucker!" she screamed.

Okay, a couple of things here. First of all, her filthy mouth was cracking me up. I wondered if that's how she always approached sex or if it was just the booze talking. Second of all, I was pretty sure this girl had just taken a shit so there was no way I was putting my mouth anywhere near that area. I decided to fake it. I climbed onto the bed and sat on my knees between her legs. I licked two fingers (I was only going to do that once) and used them to massage her clit. I tried to simulate the movements of a tongue. "Mmmmmm..." she moaned. I guessed she was buying it.

I did that for a few minutes but I was eager for the real action. I spread her legs a little wider and went for it. We both moaned as I slid my cock in. She felt great. Her pussy was so warm and wet. I felt her tits through her shirt. I was hesitant to remove her top and bra thinking I'd just have to dress her later and that would just be extra hassle. By the way, there's nothing in my rulebook that says they have to put their own clothes back on.

I'd been working up a pretty good sweat when all of a sudden her eyes pop wide open and we lock pupils for a moment. I thought for sure I was busted. Finally she screams out, "Fuck my cornhole!" At this point I wasn't sure if she meant fuck my cornhole, Jeff, or fuck my cornhole, Nick. Either way, the word cornhole didn't sound too inviting. I know a lot of guys wouldn't hesitate to take her up on it but again, she'd just taken a shit as far as I knew. The thought of sending Mr. Johnson up the same chute that fecal matter had recently used to escape made me kind of ill.

"What the fuck are you waiting for?" she screamed loud enough for the next county to hear. "Fuck my goddamn stinky ring!"

I cringed. God this girl was filthy. "Okay, okay. Just quiet down," I said. What could I do? I had to shut her up. I knew I didn't have any lube around and I didn't want to dig through her stuff (I'd feel dirty if I did something like that, you know, invasion of privacy or whatever) so I flipped her over, spread her cheeks and worked it on in without it. By the sounds she was making, she seemed to be enjoying it. And I think she enjoyed it often. It wasn't exactly tight in there if you know what I mean. I have to admit I was kind of enjoying it too.

I was pumping away at a good clip and had a good rhythm going when she screamed at me to stop. This was wacky. A part of me wished it had never happened. I pulled out and sat on my knees to wait for the next command. She turned on her side and scooted toward me. She grabbed my cock and wrapped her lips around it. I was thoroughly disgusted. I almost didn't let her do it but I didn't want her to yell again, so I caved.

It went pretty quick after that. Within seconds of entering her mouth, I blew my load. I don't know why it surprised me that she swallowed it all, but it did. She continued to suck until I was completely limp. "Thanks, baby," she said and flopped down exhausted. I felt dirty, both mentally and physically. I needed shower.

The shower cleansed my outside, but inside I still felt like shit. I couldn't even look at her lying there naked anymore. The sexy blue thong on the floor didn't seem so sexy anymore either. I was able to get that back on her without too much trouble so I attempted to slip her jeans back on as well, the fewer questions in the morning, the better. I got them all the way on but was having trouble with the buttons. I decided to leave well enough alone. I pulled the sheet and blanket up to her shoulders, kind of tucked her in and turned toward my chair-bed. "Thank you, Nick," she groggily whispered.

"Huh?" I could feel my eyes widen beyond their limits. She'd said my name this time.

"I said thanks."

"For what?" I asked with skepticism.

"Everything."

"Uh... no problem." Shit, I thought as I turned out the light and settled into the chair. What was that all about? What did she know?

I didn't sleep a wink after that. Obviously part of it was because I was sleeping in a chair, but the biggest part was that my brain wouldn't shut down. Had Anna known exactly what she was doing? Maybe she was a nympho and did this all the time. Is this why Eddie was adamant about her full bush? Maybe the same thing happened to him. Or maybe she had some contagious ass disease or something. Fuck, I'm probably going to die now. I'm going to hell at the very least. Fuck. *Fuck!* But then again, maybe I was just being paranoid. She was probably just thanking me for the ride back and the bed for the night. Yeah, that's got to be it. It's probably not, though. Shit. This was the kind of junk running through my head all night long. There was no way I was getting any sleep now.

I awoke to Anna's cell phone playing Ricky Martin's *She Bangs* as a ring tone. I guess I had finally drifted off. The last time I remembered looking at the clock it read 5:09. It was now 8:32. It took her a moment to find the phone. It was idiot-girl, Vicky, saying she'd meet her for breakfast at the diner around the corner from the motel. God, finally. Where the fuck had she been all night?

Anna sat up and smacked her lips, blew into her hand and smelled it. "Ugh. You ever get really bad morning breath?" she asked. "Mine smells like shit."

I couldn't say a word.

"You have any mouth wash?"

"In there." I pointed toward the bathroom. I stayed in the chair. My neck was killing me and I was afraid to move wrong. I'd take it slow once she left.

Anna freshened up, gathered her things and went for the door. She opened it then stopped and turned around. "Thanks again," she said. "I'm sure you had better things to do than baby-sit me your first night back."

"It's cool, I had some fun."

"Good. See you at work later."

I nodded. "Okay."

"Oh, by the way, I left something for you on the sink - just so you'll never be unprepared or anything." And with that she was gone.

I slowly got out of the chair and made my way to the bathroom. When I saw what was on the sink I almost fell over. I picked it up and took a long, hard look at a half-used tube of K-Y Jelly.

SAM SMELLS SEX

My old roommate, Dave, has this dog, Sam, that I swear can smell sex. Or maybe it's testosterone. Or semen. I'm still not quite sure, but it was a real problem for a while. Sam, by the way, is a female in case you're wondering.

I lived in the basement of this old house. The place was huge and wide open.

You entered through the kitchen and down a flight of stairs. There was no door at the top in the kitchen, but there was at the bottom which was cool because if somebody needed me and had to knock on the door, they would have to come all the way down instead of me going all the way up to see what was what.

My girlfriend, Carly, used to stay over a couple nights a week but as soon as we'd start making love, Sam would make her way down the stairs and begin to howl right outside the door. We thought it was kind of cute the first two or three times, but then it really started to

187

get on our nerves. Time didn't matter to Sam. It could be two o'clock in the morning and she would wake up, bound down the stairs and start in. She woke the other roommates and the neighbors. The police were even called on two occasions. It was kind of funny to see poor Dave standing on the porch in the middle of the night, perplexed and trying to apologize to the cops for Sam's incessant barking.

We quit doing it at my place altogether after the second police incident and it wasn't long before the whole "dog thing", as Carly put it, destroyed the relationship. She was horny all the time and wanted to screw constantly but her roommate was kind of a pain in the ass about me being at their place so much, so we couldn't do it there, or anywhere, more than a couple times a week.

That was all it took to kill the relationship, a couple weeks of sneaking around, doing it half as often and it was all over. I suggested we get a place together but that was out of the question because her parents were hard-line Christians who would never allow cohabitation before marriage. If they only knew how great their daughter was at blowjobs, but that's a whole other story. It was either the dog or her. Well, she wasn't my dog; I couldn't just get rid of her, not that I would anyway. There was nothing I could do, so it ended. Carly and I were done. I wanted to blame Sam, but she was the sweetest shepherd mix, gentle and loving toward everyone, you just couldn't stay mad at her. One look at that face and all was forgiven.

I have to admit I was as horny as Carly was so with her gone I found myself jerking off two or three times a day. But even that got Sam going. No sooner would I lie down and get into it, she would start in. Even if I tried it in the shower, without fail, there she'd be, outside my door howling her little lungs out. It got so I couldn't achieve release in my own house and I was getting pretty backed up.

Sam Smells Sex

It wasn't until a few days after Carly had left me that I came up with the "smell of sex theory". I needed to find a solution because this clearly could not go on. I decided to conduct a little experiment. I called for Sam, gave her a treat and told her to lie down. I closed the door, stood next to it and played with myself until I got hard. She stayed quiet. Okay, it wasn't just arousal or foreplay that set her off. I kept going. All of a sudden she just went off, barking to beat the band. I looked down and saw that a bead of semen was sitting in the slit of my dick. Was that it? She could smell that? I knew they trained these dogs to sniff drugs and things like that, but this was the first time I'd ever heard of a cum-sniffing dog.

Now that I had an idea what got Sam so riled up, I needed to either shut her up or find a new way to do the things I do. I became obsessed. I couldn't lock her out of the house because she would just come right back in through the doggie door and I couldn't lock her in another room because she apparently could smell right through walls. I waited until she went outside to shit then I would try to jerk off in the two or three minutes she'd be out there. This wasn't the greatest plan. Rarely did I get off in time and when I did, it was too rushed to enjoy. I was going insane. Every time I heard her move upstairs I would drop what I was doing and go see if she was going out. Nine times out of ten, she was just stretching or moving from room to room. I needed something to distract her and keep her out there longer. I fed her a tiny bit of chocolate. It made her sick and gave her the squirts something awful but at least she stayed outside most of the day and left me alone. I felt bad but I had needs damn it. I only did that once, though, because the guilt was just too much.

The next day I was back to waiting for Sam to shit on her own. As soon as I was sure she'd gone out, I hightailed it down the stairs, shoved my pants down to my ankles, flopped down on the bed and started yanking away at warp speed. What I didn't realize, though, was that in my haste I had not closed my door all the way and I was so into what I was doing (I was jerking to this girl from high school called "The Beardless Clam") that I didn't notice Sam come in.

"The Clam" had always been my ace in the hole. Her memory could get the job done in two minutes flat. I exploded. Most of the jiz formed a pool on my hand next to my thumb while the rest ran down my wrist. I had broken a sweat and maybe even a record for time. I rolled over to grab my jerk-off towel off the floor and that's when I saw Sam sitting up on her haunches, tongue out and watching, seemingly enjoying the show but best of all, not howling. I nearly jumped out of my skin. My first instinct was to cover up. I quickly grabbed for the covers but forgot that my hand had cum on it. It got all over the black comforter. I was pissed because I knew it was going to leave an ugly stain.

Sam calmly stood up and walked over to me. "Shoo! Go on!" I ordered.

She ignored me and sniffed around the sticky stuff. I kicked at her through from under the covers. "Go! Get the fuck out of here!" She was undeterred.

She started to lap it up. I was disgusted. "Oh, Jesus, no!" I cried. I tried to push her away, but she just wouldn't go. She was enjoying it.

When she was satisfied that she had gotten every little bit she apparently tried to thank me by licking my face. "Oh no you don't," I said. "No fucking way." I jumped out of bed and tried make a run for the bathroom but since I forgot my pants were still around my ankles, I only got about three feet before I fell flat on my face. Well, not flat on it, there was still enough of my face exposed to let Sam adequately show her appreciation for the salty snack.

It was somewhere around this point that I heard, "Oh my fucking God!" from across the room. I pushed Sam away long enough to see Carly standing at the door with horror in her eyes and her hands covering her mouth.

I got my own look of horror. "Oh, shit!"

Carly turned and raced up the stairs.

"Wait!" I screamed. "It's not what you think!" I scrambled to my feet, pulled up my pants and ran after her.

I caught up with her outside, just as she was getting into her car. "You're a sick fuck, you know that?" she said slamming the door.

"Let me explain," I said in desperation.

"Oh I think I've got the picture! And to think I was coming by to apologize for being too harsh!" She started the car.

"It was an accident!"

"Ugh. That's just sick!"

"No, I mean she just came in while I was jerking off!"

"I don't want to hear any more." She put the car in reverse.

"I was thinking of you while I was doing it!" I lied.

"Fuck *you*!" She stepped on the gas and burned rubber out of the driveway.

"You won't mention this to anyone will you?" I yelled as I ran after her.

She reached the street, dropped it into drive and stood on the gas. She must have gone zero to sixty in four seconds flat. "I figured out how to make Sam stop howling!" I yelled, like she could actually hear. "She just likes to watch!"

I stood in the street, alone and pathetic watching her break speed records to get away from me. I felt a presence. I looked down and there was Sam looking up at me with that cute little face of hers. If I didn't know better I'd say it almost looked as if she were smiling at me. "You know that once she tells everyone what she thinks she saw my life will be over, right?" I said.

Sam barked as if to say yes.

I shrugged my shoulders and headed for the house. "Come on, girl, let's get out of the street."

ABOUT THE AUTHOR

Vinny Smith is a southern California-based author and screenwriter. He lives with his girlfriend, Jennie, and the inspiration for *The Dog Don't Lie*, their daredevil Brussels Griffon, Murphy, who also thinks he can fly.